HENRY W

MW00567504

MIRACULOUS HEALING
and You

WHAT THE BIBLE TEACHES
WHAT YOU NEED TO KNOW

CRC Publications
Grand Rapids, Michigan

Miraculous Healing and You: What the Bible Teaches, What You Need to Know, © 1999 by CRC Publications, 2850 Kalamazoo Ave. SE, Grand Rapids, MI 49560.

Cover: *Christ Healing the Mother of Simon Peter,* J. Bridges, ex. 1818-1854; Agnew & Sons, London/Bridgeman Art Library, London/Superstock

Art (pages 8, 16, 32, 38, 48, 54, 64): SuperStock
Art (pages 72, 82): SIS

We welcome your comments. Call us at 1-800-333-8300 or e-mail us at editors@crcpublications.org.

Library of Congress Cataloging-in-Publication Data
Wildeboer, Henry, 1939-
    Miraculous healing and you : what the Bible teaches, what you need to know / Henry Wildeboer.
      p. cm.
    Includes bibliographical references (p. 95).
    ISBN 1-56212-417-X
    1. Miracles. 2. Spiritual healing. 3. Reformed Church—Doctrines. I. Title.
    BT97.2.W47   1999
    231.7'3—dc21   99-37885
                                            CIP

10 9 8 7 6 5 4 3 2 1

CONTENTS

INTRODUCTION

Joy Dampened by Pain

As I reflect on my long personal journey in the church, I am thankful that God blessed me with a simple, childlike faith that has carried over into adulthood. I have never doubted that God is *able* to perform miracles, and in my years of ministry I have regularly been reminded that God is still *willing* to do so. This conviction of God's willingness and my experiences with healings, combined with theological struggles and ministry, have created times of great joy—and times of deep pain.

Joy is dampened as I, like many others, recall painful instances when we sought God with all our hearts. Asking, watching, and believing that God would heal, we stood by the bedside to see the person die. Basic to our faith is a sovereign God who rules and guides all people, things, and events in this vast universe. But sometimes the confession "God works all things for good" is more of an aggravating theology than a joyful reality.

Cautious Searching

When God does intervene with a miracle, we tend to be cautious, even skeptical, before acknowledging God's involvement. As conservative Christians who confessionally ascribe all power to God, we fear anything out of the ordinary.

A miracle in the church community creates an environment in which it can be difficult to return to the controlled stability that was so comfortably predictable. A miraculous healing stirs up intense emotions of joy, often expressed with tears, laughter, clapping, or other expressions sometimes beyond our comfort zone. When these deep feelings are spontaneously expressed in a meticulously planned, carefully maintained worship service, some pastors feel out of control.

Likewise, pastoral ministry is deeply colored by miracles. Members want pastors to pray when they visit those who are ill. Some expect changes because of those prayers; others are shocked when they happen. In visiting other churches and talking with their pastors and leaders, I am amazed that *every* church and pastor—even those who doubt that miracles happen today—report stories of miraculous healings, which often occurred after a time of intense prayer. A few of these stories are included throughout this book.

Even when we talk about miracles, we are cautious. What answers are we really searching for when we ask, "Do we believe in miracles today?" Are we looking for an intellectual theological discussion to satisfy our curiosity? Or are we asking because we are aware of a major need for which we require God's help?

Another Step

I was reluctant to explore the area of miracles and move into a ministry of healing. My tradition did not really expect miraculous healings. Having seen others ridiculed when they emphasized the importance of prayer, I carefully weighed the risks.

In my early years of ministry, my self-image was brittle and was largely determined by what colleagues, seminary professors, and other denominational leaders thought of me. Breaking through that bondage was hard. A major healing occurred when I was released from that pressure and became more concerned with what God wanted. I discovered that one's own journey *does* play a major part in one's theology.

Finally, we are openly talking about miracles. I am pleased to participate in the discussion. I hope this book, the accompanying leader's guide, and subsequent discussions will boost faith, intensify prayer, and boldly lead many people to ask God to continue to reveal himself with "signs and wonders" that vividly portray God's reality and presence in the church today.

Allow this book to be another step in *your* journey with God. If it stretches you to believe more deeply, expect more fervently, and ask more boldly for God's fullness and presence, God will be praised, you will be blessed, and I will be thankful.

—Henry Wildeboer

Christ Curing the Epileptic Child

—Theodoor Van Loon, 1581-1667

CHAPTER 1

A JOURNEY OF LEARNING

I remember well the summer of 1963. As a twenty-three-year-old seminary student, I was assigned to be the student pastor for a small, young church in northern Alberta, Canada. The church provided a small apartment where I lived and cooked most of my meals, but I was also regularly invited to have supper with a couple I'll call Joe and Joanne. Because they had no children and loved many of the same activities I did, we often spent an open evening together. We'd go to a ballgame or an auction sale or visit another church family. At the end of some of those evenings I would be invited to my friends' home for coffee or a "snack" (a bacon-and-eggs breakfast at midnight!). Nearing the end of my summer assignment, we were enjoying what would be one of our last late-night sessions. Well after midnight, with an artery-plugging plate of food in front of me, I looked at Joanne and stated, "You two would make marvelous parents." This seemed like an obvious conclusion, since they had been exactly that to me.

Joanne looked at Joe, who had stopped eating. An awkward silence suddenly surrounded us. I felt I had blown it and wished I could pull back what I had said. It was a spontaneous comment, genuinely intended as a compliment, but one that had the opposite effect. Tears began to roll down Joanne's usually jovial face. Then Joe and Joanne shared the pain of their hearts with me. In more than sixteen years of marriage, Joanne had never been pregnant. They had done some medical consulting, but over the last five years they had given up their dream. They were resigned to believe that it was God's will that they not have children.

"Have you ever prayed to God about this?" I asked. Looking back now, I know it was a rather stupid question. Of course they had, but they had stopped praying for children during recent years. Joe and Joanne had chosen not to talk about this matter anymore—not even to God. Still, I suggested we pray. As I recall, we joined hands and prayed together rather briefly. A few days later I left that community to be married and return to seminary.

The following May, Joe called me to say that he and Joanne had been blessed with the birth of a son. I had been shocked when I had heard that they were expecting a child; I was elated when the news came that the baby had been born. The skeptic could call it a remarkable coincidence. But Joe stated it well: "God answers prayer. It's a miracle!"

That event in the beginning of my ministry experience profoundly affected my theological reflection and subsequent ministry. My childhood and my theological journey, combined with my ministry experience, removed the obstacle that assumed that miracles ceased with the closing of the Canon of Scripture. My journey is not unique. Many others—especially those who were involved in the charismatic movement of the 1970s—have traveled a similar route.

Diverse Responses

How do we respond to the subject of miracles today? Albert Einstein reportedly stated that there are only two ways to live: the first, as if nothing is a miracle; the other, as if everything is. His philosophical statement gives room for a diverse response to miracles, and Christians find themselves somewhere on the continuum from nothing to everything.

Some Christians ridicule the idea of miracles happening today. With hilarity they tell about the lady who returned from a trip to Israel. As she came through customs, she was asked about the contents of a rather large bottle in her travel bag. She explained, "Oh, that's holy water from the river Jordan." The officer took it out, opened it, smelled it, and replied, "Smells like whiskey to me." Quickly she retorted, "Isn't that amazing, another modern-day miracle!"

Others are cautious, *super*-cautious. They became that way because they were present when hopes were confidently raised that God was going to heal a friend who was ill. Those hopes were rudely shattered when, after sincere prayer and genuine faith, the healing didn't happen. "Wasn't our faith strong enough?" they wonder. The experience left questions, hurt, and a dose of fear. They now prefer to stay clear of the issue.

Many Reformed Christians prefer to avoid the topic of miracles even though some of these same people share testimonies of family members or friends who have been miraculously healed. Although some believe that these miracles may be spurious or questionable, or at least hard to verify, many do admit that miracles still occur. They do not deny the reality of miracles, but they don't know how to deal with them.

For the Pentecostal Christian, the response to a miracle, usually a healing, is "Yes, God is with us!" It's a sign of the presence of the Holy Spirit that raises the courage and confidence to meet further tests of faith or new challenges. Like a sacramental sign, the miracle confirms the truth of the gospel and the reality of God. A healing is a faith-boosting experience.

So how do we respond to the issue of miracles today? Do miracles still happen? Does God bring healing in ways other than common medical channels? If so, is there a ministry that the church should be developing? We need an opportunity to ask these honest, basic questions. The aim of this book is to do that in the light of what the Bible teaches and what the church is experiencing.

Divisive Opinions

In Christian circles, strong, often divisive, opinions prevail. Many people have taken sides with their minds made up. Some decisions are based on theological training, more on good and bad experience in the churches, and many on a mixture of both.

Fear surrounds the subject. Discussions quickly become heated debates in which emotions are aroused and tempers flare, leaving strained relationships that take a long time to heal. Heresy charges float around.

Miracles obviously occurred during Old and New Testament times. Few Bible-believing Christians challenge that. But what about today? Huge debates all through history have put God-fearing Christians on both sides of the issue. For some, the closing of the Canon and the gift of the sixty-six books of Scripture are adequate proof of the deity of Christ and the reality of God. Signs are no longer needed, and miracles no longer occur. Simple.

Others are equally convinced that miracles continued through every age, including this current, scientific century. Miracles occur where they are expected and where someone is willing to pray for them. Sometimes great faith is present (some would make that an essential precondition). At other times a miracle occurs unexpectedly to the surprise of all.

Christians line up on both sides. A growing group of Christians believes that miracles do occur today. Like many others, I grew up believing that miracles *could* happen but rarely, if ever, *did* happen. My belief has changed and developed, partially through reading, reflection, study, and ministry. Contact with other Christians, the journey of life, and a variety of miraculous experiences have all contributed. Ecumenical experiences tend to broaden and change one's perspective.

Shaped Through Ministry

After graduation from seminary, I began my pastoral ministry in the State of Washington. Work in a busy, relatively large church deflected further reflection, at least for a time. I preached, visited, taught classes, attended many meetings, and went through all the rites of passage, but I saw few conversions. Minimal ministry was done for people who were not members of the church. As in most churches, backsliders were on our rolls. I visited, prayed, begged, cajoled, and did all I could to bring them back into the church. An occasional "success" caused rejoicing and kept me going, but in my more somber moments I had to admit that as a "fisher of men" I was not successful. I spent most of my energy feeding fish and keeping their aquarium clean. Even then, I was having a tough time stopping the fish from jumping out!

My sermon preparation and personal reading of the Scriptures made me painfully aware that whatever power Jesus, the disciples, and the New Testament church had experienced was not present in my life. A few conversions and one "unusual" healing occurred, but whatever Jesus meant by "greater things than these" (John 14:12) appeared to not be happening in my ministry. Sometimes I felt that I was not doing anything significant at all even though the ministry was "going well." Good strokes, ego-boosting invitations to serve other churches, unity within the church family, and happy members would seem to be blessings enough. Yet I wondered why people in the Chamber of Commerce organization and other community groups I participated in were often more unified and happier than the members of my church.

From Experience to Introspection

Disconcerting questions were growing within me. "Is the church the empowered body of Christ, or is it simply another club?" And worse, "Am I doing what God really wants me to be doing? Is there more to it?" Nagging questions to carry around!

After five years in Washington and with many of these questions unanswered, we moved to Calgary, Alberta, Canada, to take up ministry in a Dutch-Canadian Christian Reformed Church. Two major things occurred, neither of which I expected nor initiated. But as they happened I responded. I now see those two experiences as God's response, at least partially, to a hunger that was far greater than my searching questions. Many others too were hungry for more, not knowing what that might be.

The first was a miraculous healing of a nineteen-year-old young man I'll call John. John, a member of my congregation from a neighboring community, had slipped into a deep coma because of an apparent viral infection and was taken to a large university medical center in Calgary. He had experienced a long period of very high fever. One doctor summed up John's condition with these words: "If he recovers, his brain will be like jelly." Hundreds of people rallied in prayer, and John was miraculously healed! I was directly involved and saw the miracle take place. It made me aware on a deep level that God is real, that God *does* hear the prayers of his people, and that God's hand is not shortened. This healing miracle had a profound effect on the congregation, on many other people, and on my subsequent ministry. (I first told the story of this miracle in the January 31, 1972, issue of *Calvinist Contact*, a Christian weekly newspaper. It's recounted here with permission from *Christian Courier*.)

The second event that deeply affected my spiritual and theological journey was a forty-nine-day revival in a neighboring Pentecostal church. The church was known for revival services, but this one was different in that virtually our entire membership attended at least one night or more. Many responded to altar calls at the conclusion of messages that I believed were inferior to mine. Many were "prayed over," some were "converted," others were "slain in the Spirit and received the gift of tongues." Significant miracles of healing took place. Our members were healed, but in another church! A good number returned convinced that similar signs would occur in our worship services in

---

I was born with a congenital hip defect. At that time, not much was done by way of diagnosis or correction. When I was a child, I was always told to walk straight, but I could not. While growing up, I was fairly free of pain, and eventually I received a ⅜-inch lift on my right shoe.

During my high school and college years, I developed painful back trouble. Time and time again I went to a chiropractor. The pain continued sporadically through my seminary years and afterwards. While serving my first congregation in Lebanon, Iowa, I decided to go to the nearby Mayo Clinic in Rochester, Minnesota. Doctors there decided that they would not do surgery. The best I could do, according to their advice, was to exercise the muscles and keep them in the best shape possible.

Nearly thirty years later while living in California, I attended a meeting at which the speakers were a husband and wife team from Edmonds, Washington. (The man was a mailman.) They were being used by God in a ministry of healing. The two of them laid hands on me while they thanked and praised the Lord. They made no petitions or requests. Twice my lower back bones snapped, and I was instantly healed. I did not fully realize that I was healed until the next morning when I had no more pain. I no longer needed the shoe lift. A doctor confirmed that the congenital hip defect that had plagued me for fifty-two years was healed.

Jesus is supreme, and his Spirit in us is greater than he who is in the world!

—Henry Bajema. Used by permission.

Henry Bajema pastored Christian Reformed churches in Lebanon, Iowa; Cincinnati, Ohio; Hudsonville, Michigan; Lacombe, Alberta (First); Volga, South Dakota; Hanford, California; and Holland Center, South Dakota. Following his retirement, he served as visiting pastor at Sunshine Community Church in Grand Rapids, Michigan. Henry and his wife, Ruth, live in Belmont, Michigan.

response to prayer. To be sure, the opposite response was also present. Some called to say, "Tell our members not to go there." In no uncertain terms, some said, "What is happening there is straight from the devil!"

As we prayed more specifically and boldly about critical needs, things began to happen. Other changes—different, but equally as dramatic as the healing miracles—were taking place. A father went to his teenage son and sobbingly asked for forgiveness for being harsh and impatient for all of that son's life. Husbands apologized to wives. People who seemed to only be going through the motions of worship began to ask for more meaningful worship. Many wanted more praise, some became deeply convicted about the importance of witnessing for Christ, others asked for prayer meetings. I saw cautious, conservative Christians, many of whom were known for their thriftiness, become instant tithers! Some who vigorously debated the need for Christian schools were now rather suddenly convinced that their children needed a Christ-centered education. Miracles!

Theological Reflections on the Run

We, pastor and congregation, embarked on a ten-year roller-coaster ride. Many struggled with questions similar to those that commonly surface in the teenage years: "Is God real? Is there more to the Christian faith and reality than what my church is experiencing?" And this question: "Can a more traditional church live with a significant group of members with charismatic experiences who in their worship praise God with a new zeal and who pray with great expectations?"

Many in the congregation were not afraid to pray for miracles. When they were sick, they asked for the elders to come as instructed in James 5:14. Sometimes, to our surprise and amazement, God healed. In several instances, surgeries already scheduled were canceled after anointing with oil and prayer. But in other instances where equally fervent prayer, strong faith, and "bold claims" were present, no healing or improvement took place.

During the ups and downs of this period in my spiritual journey, I developed the following convictions:

• Although Reformed theology and practice is thoroughly biblically based, our involvement in the area of prayer and healing has been minimal.

Reformed Christians have much to contribute to others, but they also have much to learn from them, particularly in the areas of prayer, spiritual gifts, "stepping out in faith," and expecting great things from God. As Reformed Christians we have not always been open to learning from others or allowing them to help us. Contact with other Christians is enriching.

- The subject of miracles is often overemphasized, both by those who experience miracles and by those who don't.

Miracles are part of God's grace and are significant to the people who experience them. In the realm of the kingdom of God, no miracle is greater than the resurrection of Christ. Let no one underestimate the miracle of regeneration or conversion. Why be surprised when the God who converts self-centered individuals with hard, calloused hearts into pliable, tender, unselfish servants also heals bodily ailments? Healing is relatively minor compared to the bigger miracle that has occurred.

- Miracles, and especially healings, are more than an academic, doctrinal issue.

Miracles are delicate experiences because they deal with life, illness, and death. We may experience nervousness, tension, and even fear as we encounter these issues. It is an awesome experience for the insignificant self to be aware of the presence of a majestic God, yet know that what one does and says at such moments may have life-changing consequences. That reality stops ministry from becoming trivial. The subject warrants treatment with tender care. The final word has been neither spoken nor written. With openness of heart and spirit we enter this journey with the confidence that God will enrich all of us.

Once again we ask: "Do miracles occur today? How do we view them?" These questions warrant a response. Our response requires a mutual listening to the Scriptures, the source of life and instruction. Before doing that in subsequent chapters, we'll define *miracle* in chapter 2.

Healing of the Paralytic

—Artist Unknown, 1560-90

WHAT IS A MIRACLE?

In our culture the word *miracle* is tossed about indiscriminately. It is used to explain the mundane in statements like "It's a miracle that I made it to work on time!" or "It's a miracle that we made it to the gas station without running out of gas." Or the word might be used in a more serious vein: "After many prayers, my mother was healed of cancer. It was a miracle!" Mention of the word *miracle* often brings to mind a story in which the unusual or unexpected happened. It may be a sudden turn in an illness or a change in circumstances with an apparent "streak of good luck."

Miracles, though common to Christianity, are not limited to it. New Age adherents, Buddhists, Native Americans, and Aboriginal Canadians are among those who have prayers, rites, and rituals for healing miracles. Many people not involved in the Christian church speak of miracles, usually in relation to healing.

We cannot avoid the subject of miracles when we read the Bible. The Scriptures present a vast assortment of miracles: the lame walk, the deaf hear, the blind see, the leper regains the use of lost limbs, and the dead are raised. Miracles other than healings occur: bread and fish are multiplied, water becomes wine, a little jug of oil fills barrels, and a little jar of flour has enough for many meals. Though the earth opens its jaws and swallows people, hungry lions can't touch their evening's dinner of tender human flesh. A fiercely overheated oven fries the attendants who stoke it but fails to singe the young men who walk around in it. Some sites are miraculously flooded, some cities are burned out of existence. Another caves in after people blowing trumpets walk around it a few times. One day the sun stands still; another day, much later, darkness at noon stops activities for three hours. A threatening storm is calmed when told to do so. A school of fish manages to escape nets all night only to be nudged to the other side of a boat where they are caught in the morning. At another time a fish with enough money in its mouth to pay the taxes is caught.

By Definition, A Miracle Is . . .

Miracles have a long history in culture and in the Scriptures. The words *sign* (*oth* in Hebrew), *wonders* (*teras* in Greek), and *power* (*dunamis* in Greek) describe miracles throughout the Old Testament. The New Testament writers used a variety of words to describe miracles, but most commonly used two words: *semeion* (signs or wonders) and *dunamis* (power, ability, or miracle). In the gospel of

John, the word *semeion* is usually translated "miracle" or, in the NIV, "miraculous sign" (see John 2:11, 23; 3:2; 6:26; 7:31; 9:16; 11:47; 12:37). Earlier English translations also used "mighty works" (see Matt. 7:22; 11:20-21; 13:54, 58; Mark 6:2, 5, 11; Luke 10:13; 19:37). *Thauna,* the common Greek word for miracles, is used in the New Testament to describe the wonder and admiration of people responding to the miracle rather than to describe the miracle itself (Harper, *The Healings of Jesus,* p. 126).

But how is the word defined and understood in our culture? As you'll observe from the definitions included here, each authority views the word *miracle* through different windows.

- *Merriam-Webster's Collegiate Dictionary* defines *miracle* as (1) an extraordinary event manifesting divine intervention in human affairs; (2) an extremely outstanding or unusual event, thing, or accomplishment; (3) *Christian Science*: a divinely natural phenomenon experienced humanly as the fulfillment of spiritual law.

- Augustine (*On the Profit of Believing,* No. 34) deems a miracle to be something that is difficult or unusual, above the hope or beyond the power of those who are there. For him, it is simply something that we don't understand and that causes us to wonder.

- Ernst and Luise Keller (*Miracles in Dispute,* p. 16) credit God and give this definition specifically geared toward Christians: "A miraculous act is a happening or deed which can be effected by no natural cause, being above the settled and recognized laws of nature; and which can hence only be attributed to God, the creator and Lord of nature; for example, the resurrection of a dead body."

- Robert A. Larmer, professor of philosophy at the University of New Brunswick, takes a more philosophical approach. He believes a miracle has four basic characteristics (*Water into Wine,* p. 5):

  (1) A miracle is a physical event which is beyond the ability of an unaided nature to produce.

  (2) A miracle is brought about by a rational agent.

  (3) It is an event of an extraordinary kind.

  (4) It has religious significance.

  Larmer adds this summary: "A miracle, then, is an event which nature would not produce on its own; it is supernaturally caused and involves an overriding of the usual course of nature . . . brought about by a rational agent not bound by nature, acting upon nature to produce an event which would not have otherwise occurred" (p. 5). Larmer says that, though there is a rational mind behind miracles, one cannot really prove conclusively that God is that mind, even though a miracle has religious significance.

- C. S. Lewis emphasizes that miracles suspend the laws of nature rather than override them (*The Grand Miracle*, pp. 2-3). Joseph was going to put Mary away because he knew that in the normal course of nature pregnancy results from sexual intercourse. In Joseph's mind, Mary had been unfaithful, and rather than embarrass her he would drop her quietly. After God informed Joseph that the Holy Spirit had suspended the laws of nature and had impregnated Mary directly, Joseph changed his plans and proceeded with the marriage. For Lewis, "The experience of a miracle in fact requires two conditions. First we must believe in a normal stability of Nature, which means we must recognize that the data offered by our senses recur in regular patterns. Secondly, we must believe in some reality beyond Nature."

Who's Shaping the Miracle?

Definitions of the word *miracle* usually include the idea that someone or something is guiding or shaping the miracle. Who is it that comes from "outside of nature" or "overrides nature"? If miracles seem purposeful and rational, then *who* is the rational mind that brings them about?

To Christians, the rational mind is God, the Creator. *Any* miracle is the work of God, because God is the Almighty one involved with *all* things, including miracles that happen to non-Christians. Christians see the hand of God because they believe in God; the Christian gives credit to the God of heaven and earth and views the miracle as confirmation of God's existence.

But the occurrence of a miracle, even one that results from prayer, does not for all people empirically prove the existence of God. Various religions have rituals of prayer seeking healing from their gods, and many report that healings occur. Like Christians, members of each religion praise their god and believe their god performed the miracle. Buddhists credit Buddha; Islamic people praise Allah; Hindus honor a host of gods. For the agnostic, the miracle proves little, if anything.

Ours is not unlike the time of Jonah, when each person "cried out to his own god" (Jonah 1:5). They hoped that one of them—it didn't really matter which one—would stop the raging storm. When that didn't work and the captain later found Jonah sleeping in the hold of the ship, he let him have it! "How can you sleep? You call on *your* god." The captain thought that maybe Jonah's god was the one who could stop the storm. The sailors drew lots and trusted the gods to let the lot fall on the one who was the cause of the storm. Jonah was picked; the man running from God was singled out. Although they hated to do it, the sailors dumped Jonah overboard as a sacrifice to the god of the storm. They hoped that this god would be appeased and would stop the raging sea, a trade-off—better to lose one than for all to be lost. It worked! The *NIV Study Bible* explains that "the sailors acknowledged that the God of Israel was in control of the present events" but that "there is no evidence that the sailors renounced all other gods" (notes, v. 16). They all had gods, believed in them, and were convinced that their gods had the power to create storms and to quiet them.

Common Characteristics of Miracles

Miracles have two common characteristics:

- First, a miracle seems unnatural in that nature would not produce it on its own in the normal course of events. It seems to override nature or even to be contrary to it.

- Second, most people view miracles, especially miracles of healing, as *something good*. This means that someone loving and good is shaping events or situations to bring about something better.

Personally, I believe that miracles were irrelevant and unnecessary before the fall. There was no sin, suffering, or death. Forgiveness was not needed, healings did not exist, and extending life or raising the dead were unknown concepts. After the fall into sin, miracles appeared as acts of God in which God intervened in events or situations by changing normal, natural processes. These events are considered miracles precisely because they are unnatural or supernatural and almost always defy rational explanation. "Praise the Lord!" is often the spontaneous expression of astonishment and fascination in response to a miracle.

It's a miracle when something painful, frightening, or ominous is changed for the better. Because we consider miracles good, we believe that someone good who loves us, knew our need, and understood our specific situation changed events to turn out for our good. For the Christian, sin, suffering, and death are unnatural. As the Spirit of the Lord works to recreate original order, miracles of healing are a natural part of the reconciling, redeeming work of God.

Miracles and Faith

Finally, there is the matter of faith. Jesus frequently raised the issue as he healed the sick, demonstrated his power over nature, and forgave sins. He often praised those who had faith. When he healed the man who couldn't walk, Jesus saw the boldness of the man and his friends as evidence of their faith (Mark 2:1-12). To the woman who touched his cloak, Jesus said, "Daughter, your faith has healed you. Go in peace and be freed from your suffering" (Mark 5:34).

But Jesus' healings were not limited to those who had faith. The stories of the multitudes that came to Jesus for healing included many who undoubtedly had no faith in him as the Messiah. Perhaps motivated by pain and desperation, they came saying, "What is there to lose?" Mark tells a story of such desperation (9:14-32). A father had tried everything to find relief for his son, who was possessed by an evil spirit. Jesus rebuked the lack of faith that teachers of the law displayed, asking, "O unbelieving generation, how long shall I stay with you?" (v. 19). Then he questioned the father's doubt, explaining that it wasn't a matter of what God *could* do but whether the father had faith to believe that Jesus could heal his son. Even the disciples lacked sufficient faith and understanding of the power of prayer to be able to drive out the evil spirit (vv. 18, 28-29). But the boy was healed!

A number of the miracle stories in the gospels make no mention of faith whatsoever. The widow of Nain (Luke 7:11-17) meets Jesus as she walks in the funeral procession to bury her dead son. Christ's heart goes out to her and in compassion he orders the dead boy to get up. No mention of anyone's faith is made. But the absence of faith was a hindrance in Jesus' hometown. He did not perform many miracles in Nazareth because "of their unbelief" (Matt. 13:58). At times the lack of faith hindered and seemed to hold back the work of the Lord, but nowhere in Scripture is faith demanded as a prerequisite to healing.

These illustrations of the relationship between faith and miracles are a comfort to the Christian. God can work wherever we are in our faith journey. People open to miracles often experience them. Miracles make us humbly grateful. They refresh our faith and deepen our confidence in God, who is real and who takes a personal interest in our lives. During tough times, which inevitably come to all Christians, we look back, recall, and remember the intervening hand of God moving directly to bring healing and wholeness. At such times, the memory of a miracle encourages us to continue to trust, even when everything else dictates throwing in the towel.

A Miracle or Mere Coincidence?

Miracles confirm the reality of God for the believer. A person may have been a believer for many years; yet a miracle brings a new, vital reality that enriches one's life and deepens one's faith. The miracle is a fresh revelation from God that creates a deep assurance that the believer is God's beloved. Though the Christian may know that a miracle is part of the new creation, he or she is still surprised with joy, especially if the miracle involves a personal healing or the restoration of a close family member or friend. The impact is deep and often long-lasting; someone who experiences a miracle is likely to never be the same again.

Agnostics or skeptics looking for objective, scientific proof will debate miracles or call them coincidences. As Christians, we are to be sensitive that something so obviously brought to us by the hand of God may well appear to be a coincidence to other people.

Coincidences do occur in our lives. For example, my wife and I camped in a small Alberta campground some 1,860 miles (3,000 km) from our home. As we talked to the campers next to us, we learned they were neighbors living within two blocks of our home—amazingly coincidental but neither unnatural nor supernatural.

By contrast, in 1981 my daughter and I went to a professional football game in Calgary, Alberta. In a crowd of some twenty thousand people, I ended up sitting next to Billy Graham, who had come to check out the stadium for a

---

I remember her well. Mariann was one of the first patients in my medical career. She came to see me because, as she confidently said, "I'm pregnant!" Having read her medical chart, I proceeded to take her history. Mariann began by telling me how for nine years she and her husband had longed for a child but that for all these years she hadn't conceived.

When I asked Mariann what made her think that she could be pregnant now, she explained that she was a Christian. Some three months earlier a friend had prayed over her. Mariann had injured her ankle some time before, and it was still painful. She also suffered from high blood pressure and took medication to treat it. When her friend prayed for her, Mariann felt a tingling sensation in her body and knew that God had touched her. The pain left her instantaneously. Confident that her hypertension was no longer a problem, she also stopped taking her medication. (Her blood pressure was normal when I checked it.)

Mariann told me that soon after the prayer experience, she began to have her first menstrual period in nine years. She came to see me because her next period was two weeks late. Thus she concluded that she must be pregnant. And indeed, she was!

I recall describing this remarkable turn of events to my colleagues. Some of them, having excluded God from their view of reality, were skeptical and assigned the matter to coincidence.

Sometimes I think a coincidence is a miracle in which God prefers to remain anonymous. However, in this case, I felt God had chosen not to go incognito. Later, after Mariann had delivered a healthy baby boy, she told me that this miracle led her father to become a Christian.

—As told to Henry Wildeboer by the physician. Used by permission.

crusade to begin two days later. That's a good example of a coincidence. But now add to it the fact that *the very same morning* I had openly said to a colleague, "I really would like to meet Billy Graham!" Some might call this "an *amazing* coincidence." An expressed desire, fulfilled the same day, made it more than coincidental to me. I pictured God chuckling to himself and saying, "Watch me work this out." We know God delights in giving us the desires of our hearts. Occasionally, like any parent, God enjoys spoiling us.

No miracle can empirically prove the existence of God in such a vivid, clear way that an unbeliever has to believe. Amazingly, right after Christ miraculously fed thousands of people with seven loaves of bread and a few fish (Mark 8:1-9), the Pharisees questioned him and asked "for a sign from heaven" (8:11), of all things! This example clearly shows that if our eyes are not open, miracles have no convincing power. No miracle in itself converts. Those whose eyes were open saw the Messiah. Others, though they witnessed the same miracle, saw nothing. It didn't matter that just prior to feeding the four thousand, Jesus had healed a man who couldn't hear (7:31-35) and that shortly after he healed the eyes of a man who was blind (8:22-26). The Pharisees' hearts were closed, their ears were deaf, their eyes were blind. Miracles did not convince everyone in the time of Christ; they do not do so today.

Miracles are helpful, supportive, and affirming, especially for searching Christians. The very miracle of salvation is the delicate, precious work of God. The inner testimony of the Holy Spirit softens our hearts and nurtures faith in God until we can no longer escape the fact that God loves us. We find ourselves wanting to respond and to discover the reality of this biblical truth: "Anyone who comes to [God] must believe that he exists and that he rewards those who earnestly seek him" (Heb. 11:6).

Adam and Eve   —Albrecht Dürer, 1504

CHAPTER 3

WHY DO MIRACLES OCCUR?

"Why does God perform a miracle in one instance and not in another?" we ask. That's a tough question to answer. But the underlying question is this: "Why does God perform miracles at all?" The answer lies in acknowledging that conflict and war plague the creation. Satan declared war on all that God made to be good, wholesome, and beautiful. The conflict developed long ago.

Conflict in the Kingdom

The Old Testament story begins with the amazing miracle of creation. (We'll discuss this miracle in more detail in Chapter 4.) God spoke and out of nothing the world, seas, land, plants, animals, and people came into being. There was harmony, balance, beauty, and a variety of foods for survival and enjoyment. It was all very good.

Sin entered the scene in Genesis 3. Tranquil, innocent gardeners were deceptively invited to become wise like God and to know good *and* evil. They succumbed and ate from the one tree forbidden by God. Surely God didn't really mean that they couldn't!

But God did! Adam and Eve, representing the entire human race, lost their innocence, their uninhibited nature, and their tranquil place in paradise. Since that fall into sin, human nature has been in conflict with nature rather than in harmony with it. Abraham Kuyper, a well-known Dutch pastor, theologian, philosopher, and politician, believes that the curse of sin has weakened humanity so that it no longer has control of nature, which has increased in power. Kuyper states that

> the human race, stricken with fear, gradually transferred the adoration that is reserved for the living God to nature. These fears did not arise when nature was in restful repose, but only when it is in a state of turbulence and agitation.

> —Abraham Kuyper, *You Can Do Greater Things Than Christ*, p. 6.

Creation, earlier under the dominion of God's children, has turned on them and is now able to destroy them. Kuyper elaborates the far-reaching consequences of the fall (pp. 7-8):

> Perhaps it is best to think of nature as having gone berserk, because of the weight of the curse under which it had to labour. . . . Just like a berserk person, nature has its moments of calm and quiet, but this is

often interrupted by periods of violence and anger that stir up all creation and threaten destruction everywhere. The earth quakes; cyclones pick up homes and hurl them down to the ground; tempestuous gales anger the ocean waves; rivers burst beyond their banks. At such times, it may seem as if all nature is hell-bent on destruction. The curse has totally transformed nature into an ominous threat. What used to be peaceful has become violent. Plants sprout thorns and thistles. Animals have become wild and roam about devouring their fellows. Sickness and pestilence abound everywhere.

In the curse expressed to the serpent representing Satan, God predicts a long battle that will end with Satan's defeat: "And I will put enmity between you and the woman, and between your offspring and hers; he will crush your head, and you will strike his heel" (Gen. 3:15). Ultimately the worst Satan will accomplish is to strike the heel of Christ, the woman's seed. Satan has done that with boundless energy. The prophecy concludes with the promise of grace that declares the victory of Christ. You will nip at the heel of the seed of the woman, but watch out—the seed will crush your *head*.

God created a good world in which God and his people would keep the garden by sharing the rhythm of work and rest. They would work as partners in the constant spirit of Sabbath rest. But all that changed. The relationship became strained. Their cooperative ruling of the creation was severely damaged. The consequences—pain, sweat, thorns, thistles, and pests—ultimately would lead to physical death, which inevitably would follow the spiritual death already experienced. Satan spares no effort to turn people against God. He entices us with temptations that promise happiness now instead of the pain of delayed gratification. The seductions of our basic nature and the power of a secular, self-centered world work with Satan to make a formidable team to distract us from loving the one who made us.

Our fear of nature and its power have led the human race to fear God. And through miracles, God shows us that he is more powerful than the mightiest acts of nature. Kuyper states,

> It is in this context that the need for miracles arose. . . . The impression nature made upon the human race was so overwhelming that it destroyed human courage. Whenever God would show signs and miracles that so brilliantly displayed his power over nature, then fear for nature would go on retreat, and God becomes once again a refuge and rock for his children (p. 9).

God formed the creation, sin deformed it, but God is reforming it through the transforming work of Christ. The prophecy of Genesis 3:15 is more than a mere prediction; it puts the wheels in motion for the original creation, now seemingly lost, to be restored. The work has started! Miracles are signs that the kingdom of God, here now in microcosm, will come in fullness. A new day will come when all darkness, fear, tension, distrust, bondage, sweat, and opposition will be replaced with light, love, peace, trust, and security. Tensions will cease, the wolf and lamb will eat together, and the lion's carnivorous nature will no longer be feared (Isa. 65:25). Work will again be pure pleasure as men and women, sharing full equality, live in cooperation and harmony rather than in competition and distrust.

The rest of the Bible unwraps the prophecy of Genesis 3:15. God reveals himself as a Father who desires a relationship of love with his children. God's faithfulness is expressed in covenant-keeping. God delights in our love and faithfulness, our expressions of thankful obedience for what he has done. Throughout the Bible, God provides glimpses of the restored creation—through servants and prophets in the Old Testament and especially, but not solely, through the chief prophet and high priest, Jesus Christ, in the New Testament. Satan's determination to dishonor God, and the sovereign God's determination to redeem his creation, sets the stage for the battles of kingdoms. Unless we see this bigger picture of kingdoms in conflict, we cannot understand miracles.

A New Kingdom Is Here and Coming

"The kingdom of God" or "the kingdom of heaven" was proclaimed by John the Baptist (Matt. 3:2) and by Jesus (Matt. 4:17). Neither explained what they meant. It was understood. The kingdom of God is the realm over which the King exercises authority. It's the realm where God's principles reign.

This concept was deeply imbedded in the hearts and minds of people who heard it; it brought an immediate response from them. The prophets spoke of the kingdom as a new day to come when men and women would live together in peace. In Jewish history, this kingdom meant hope for the future associated with messianic expectation. Though struggles continued to assault God's people, harbingers of victory surrounded them.

A new day was coming! H. Ridderbos developed this theme extensively in his book *The Coming of the Kingdom* (p. 3ff.). We'll look at three of the signs that announce the presence of this new day.

A Covenant Relationship

First, God has made it possible for a sinful, imperfect human race to have a relationship with a perfect God. In the Old Testament, God established a covenant (friendship) relationship with his people. God would be their God and Father; they would be his people. God would lead and provide; they would trust and obey. God's people failed many times; God never did. God kept his word with his people even when they chose to disobey, dishonor, or ignore God. Their disobedience, along with God's love and justice, led to the provision of a Savior in the New Testament. Christ has made possible salvation that is to be fully realized in glory, but the peace and joy that come from being reconciled with God is a *present* reality for his people.

A Defeated Enemy

Second, though Satan does everything possible to deceive and to destroy, he is a defeated enemy. The prophecy in Genesis 3:15 predicts that Satan will be crushed. This by no means stops him from trying to deceive and destroy God's

---

I think it started in 1984. That period of my life is hard to remember. I was attending a growing church and belonged to a Christian young adult group. On the outside everything seemed fine; on the inside I was in constant pain.

About that time, I read a book about a person who worshiped Satan before becoming a Christian. As I reflected about the book, I wished for more power and prestige. I wanted it all: money, position, possessions, and power, and the things that flow out of that. I concluded that if God would not give me these things, Satan would. I remember well the night when I prayed specifically and loudly to the devil for the first time. I vowed to serve Satan if he would bless me and get me a job at General Motors.

I didn't think much about what I had done that night. During the next few months my life seemed normal. I continued to attend church and the young adult group. On February 15, 1985, I started a new job at General Motors. I was thrilled to have a stable job with a good salary.

A few months later I began to have regular visions of an old man talking to me. He was telling me about things I could become. "Neat!" I thought. "I've never had this before." As I continued to listen to this man, I began to date more often, but both my attitude and my behavior on some of those dates were wrong. I also started to think of things that would injure others, and then they would actually happen.

Except to a few of my female friends, I seemed well composed. I still attended church and young adult activities. I believed in God, but something inside was controlling me. I became more afraid. I got angry for no reason. My eyes, which became black like strangers staring back at me in the mirror, actually scared me at times.

people. In the Old Testament, Satan's activities are mostly underground. Battles occur for God's people on the way to the promised land. More struggles surface when they get there. God-fearing saints like Noah, Abraham, Isaac, Jacob, Moses, Saul, David, Solomon, and a host of others all struggled with the dark sides of their characters. The common fingerprints of Satan were found in each of their lives and continue to be found in ours. He deceives each one individually and all of us corporately. Satan sows dissent between nations and brings destruction to God's creation. All of it is a flagrant attack upon God, who made all things beautiful.

When the Messiah appeared, Satan knew his days were numbered. He attacked with vicious desperation. Christ came to destroy the control and power

---

During my more reflective moments, I admitted to myself that I did not like what I was becoming. I cried out to God and began to talk to others. One night while talking to a friend, I started to cry. He advised me to see Pastor Henry.

As I drove to the church on October 28, 1985, the old man insisted on telling me that I did not need to go. Only by the grace of God did I make it to the church. When I related my experiences to Pastor Henry, it didn't take him long to discern what had happened. He called the intern pastor to join us, and the two laid hands on me and prayed for me. They asked me to renounce my vow to Satan. Before I did so, weird voices responded from within me, and my mouth drooled and foamed. After they prayed, I felt weak and knew that the evil spirit controlling me was gone. I left the church feeling completely empty and clean. I rejoiced that God loved me so much and had never left me during my time away from him. I felt a new peace and freedom.

After being delivered, I thought my life would be great as a God-fearing man serving my Lord. Though warned, I did not know that the devil would hang on—tenaciously! I was sorely tempted, and for the next five years partook in a lifestyle of which I am not proud.

Today I am free in Christ! I am deeply thankful, and I praise God that he never forsook me but continued to love me even when I was far from him.

—Ed. Used by permission.

Note: Some may refer to Ed's experience in the pastor's office as a "power encounter," a phrase that became popular during the growth of the charismatic movement in the 1970s. It was used to describe the encounter that occurred when the Spirit of God confronted the evil spirits controlling minds and bodies and was commonly used by John Wimber and others from Vineyard Fellowships.

that Satan had over the kingdom of darkness. When Jesus initiated his ministry, he was led into the wilderness to be tempted by Satan (Matt. 4:1-11). It was showdown time. Satan invited Christ to take a shortcut to victory. Jesus could have gained the kingdoms of this world *without pain* if he had just once bowed to Satan. The deception? What Satan promised as a victory was in reality a sure defeat for the kingdom of God. Christ's entire ministry was a struggle between God's kingdom of light and Satan's kingdom of darkness. It began with the wilderness temptations by Satan in person. It concluded on the cross with the criminal's invitation, "Aren't you the Christ? Save yourself and us!" (Luke 23:39).

All four gospels are filled with stories of the conflict in which miracles revealed Christ's power. Demons who bound, crippled, and destroyed were cast out. The gift of healing was a similar assault on Satan's destructive work. Christ's miracles of healing and his message of forgiveness revealed that he came to bring glory to God, destruction to Satan, and restoration to the creation. Death, illness, suffering, starvation, injustice, imprisonment, and demonization were all unnatural. They were not part of the original created order. Miracles were not unnatural; sin and suffering and death were. The gift of salvation restored people into the wholeness that Satan had ruptured. Miracles were clear demonstrations that the kingdom of God had arrived and that the end of Satan's terror was approaching. His days were numbered, his doom was sure.

After the disciples returned from a successful mission, Jesus said he "saw Satan fall like lightning from heaven" (Luke 10:18). When Jesus was accused of driving out demons by the power of Satan, he explained that no one could enter a "strong man's house and carry off his possessions unless he first ties up the strong man" (Matt. 12:29). Satan's head was crushed on the cross; his defeat was confirmed with the resurrection. Before he ascended, Christ instructed his disciples to carry on his mission and gave them the power to do so (Acts 1:8). This meant speaking his words and doing his works. The mandate was never withdrawn; the assignment remains the same for the church today.

What about Satan? Did he quit or resign? No! He opposed the apostles and has plagued and assaulted God's people through all subsequent history. All predictions and indications reveal that he will continue to do so as long as God allows him to exist. In the meantime, Christians, though deeply committed to Jesus, are faced with the ongoing struggles of life, sometimes seemingly even more than those who are flagrant unbelievers. (Psalm 73 gives a clear Old Testament example of a godly man watching the ungodly prosper.) Christians suffer as they face sickness and sorrow, turmoil and tension, conflict and confusion, and eventually they succumb to the last enemy, death. Then they are set free.

Satan's power will end with the return of Jesus Christ. The view that the kingdom is already here, although not yet fully, helps Christians understand that they are not spared from the tremendous suffering that surrounds this world's inhabitants. Simply put, even though we are in Christ, we are not immune to suffering, sickness, or death. We are not spared Satan's temptations, nor do we escape his seductive invitations to take the route of self indulgence and bypass the road of cross-bearing and self-denial. The stakes are high as Satan, the mortally wounded lion, rages, lashes out, and devours whomever is near.

If we didn't know the *good news* that Satan's days are short and his assaults temporary, we would be overwhelmed by the strain of constant turmoil. Even so, there are times when the pain causes tired sighs as the Christian plods on, crying, "I can't take this anymore!" To exhausted, defeated, tired Christians, God may well give a sign to confirm his presence. In the early church, God performed miracles as signs and reminders that his kingdom is here and coming. Nothing indicates that God has stopped giving those signs today.

God's Kingdom Come

Third, miracles are Old and New Testament signs that God's kingdom is here. Miracles show that the kingdom is present here, but they are also a foretaste of what is to come in fullness. If disasters, plagues, disease, and death are signs of the battle between light and darkness, then stilling the storm, halting an epidemic, healing the sick, and raising the dead demonstrate renewal and re-creation. The healed would become sick again, those raised from death would die again; still the miracles would manifest the coming of the kingdom of heaven. H. Ridderbos develops this theme of miracles as signs in *The Coming of the Kingdom*.

During Christ's ministry, miracles demonstrated that Jesus is the son of God. Jesus came to teach and preach the kingdom of God; the miracles were signs that supported his messages and warnings. This becomes obvious when we look at New Testament miracles.

Bible-believing Christians do not debate whether miracles occurred in New Testament times. But do they still occur today? That is the bigger question, intensely debated. Before adding to that discussion, we will look at miracles in both the Old and New Testaments.

Elijah Restoring the Widow's Son

—Ford Madox Brown, 1821-1893

MIRACLES AND THE OLD TESTAMENT

We noted in chapter 2 that the words *sign, wonder,* and *power* are used in the Bible to describe miracles. These words often appear together in various combinations in the Old Testament. The word *sign* (*oth* in Hebrew) first appears in Genesis 1:14, where lights are to serve as "signs to mark seasons and days." A sign serves as visual identification by which something is recognized. In Exodus 31:13, God tells Moses to tell the Israelites to observe Sabbaths as a "sign between me and you for the generations to come." Even though miracles are not as common in Old Testament times as in New Testament stories, miracles certainly did occur and are recorded in the Old Testament.

The Miracle of Creation

The creation miracle described in Genesis 1 is indeed the handiwork of God. "In the Old Testament, the Hebrew word for *create* is used only of divine, never of human, activity" (the *NIV Study Bible* notes for Gen. 1:1). This truth is reiterated in Isaiah 45:18:

> For this is what the LORD says—he who created the heavens, he is God; he who fashioned and made the earth, he founded it; he did not create it to be empty, but formed it to be inhabited—he says: "I am the LORD, and there is no other."

God created the earth to be *inhabited.* In Genesis 2 we're told that God places the created human being, a male, in a vast garden. Adam is given the assignment to work the garden, to take care of it, and to eat from it, with the exception of one tree. God realizes that the male does not work well alone. Adam is lonely and incomplete and does not fully portray the image of God. The Father, in Trinitarian consultation, decides to share the precious gift of union and communion with humankind. The creation miracle continues as God takes a rib from the first man and builds a woman around it. As her father, God walks her down the aisle and unites her with the man in the first-ever wedding ceremony. God forms the first husband and wife team. Uninhibited by clothes and shame, Adam and Eve happily work their garden. It's a very peaceful and happy scene. All creation sings; "the skies proclaim the work of his hands" (Ps. 19:1).

The very first page of the Scriptures calls the reader to decide how to respond to the issue of miracles. The Bible presents the creation of heaven and earth as the miraculous work of God. The way one deals with it sets the stage for how one

Pearl Van Vleit suffers from macular degeneration, a leading cause of blindness in the elderly. In January 1997, Pearl became the first person in the United States to receive a fetal-cell retinal transplant in an effort to restore her sight. . . . Two years later, Pearl reports she has recovered 40 percent of the vision in her left eye.

Dr. J. Terry Ernst performed the surgery at the University of Chicago Medical Center. Ernst, chair of the university's ophthalmology department, is astonished at Pearl's recovery of color recognition. Pearl had been told that the surgery would probably restore only her ability to see black or white.

When Ernst asked for her reaction, Pearl said, "It's God's miracle. I'm not underestimating your expertise, Dr. Ernst, but God used your expertise for this surgery."

Ernst commented, "Pearl, you want to give God all the credit, but I'd like to give the fetal cells part of the credit."

Pearl answered, "God created those too."

Ernst replied, "I can't win."

—Adapted from Martin LaMaire, "Fetal-Transplant Patient Recovers Part of Eyesight," *The Banner,* April 26, 1997, p. 6. Used by permission.

Pearl Van Vliet is a member of Calvin Christian Reformed Church, Oak Lawn, Illinois. At age 83, she volunteers one day a week at the University of Chicago Medical Center, where she answers phones and briefs patients prior to surgery.

deals with the rest of the Scriptures. To replace God's involvement as architect, designer, engineer, and builder with a belief that creation came about by chance through the random, gradual development of evolution takes a huge leap of faith. I find that as hard to believe as to be convinced that a watch or a computer came together over years in a chance-directed evolutionary process. Compared to the complexities of a balanced world sustained in a balanced solar system that in turn is sustained in a balanced universe, the computer is relatively simple.

As we saw in chapter 3, the miracle of creation was spoiled, and now God's kingdom is in conflict with Satan. As the story of redemption unfolds, God continues to perform signs and wonders throughout Old Testament times.

During the Life of Moses

Signs appeared frequently during Moses' life after God called him to deliver the Israelites out of Egypt. Moses went back to Egypt but was fearful about his assignment, especially when he learned he had to go to Pharaoh and demand the people's release. Because Moses had firsthand experience living with Pharaoh, he knew his request would not be welcomed. So Moses asked, "Who am I to do this?" God answered, "I will be with you. And this will be the sign to you that it is I who have sent you: When you have brought the people out of Egypt, you will worship God on this mountain" (Ex. 3:12). God also said, "So I will stretch out my hand and strike the Egyptians with all the wonders that I will perform among them" (v. 20).

Moses was still hesitant and asked again, "What if they do not believe me?" (4:1). God answered by giving him two signs: the staff thrown on the ground became a snake, and the hand put inside his coat turned white with leprosy (vv. 2-7). God told Moses, "If they do not believe you or pay attention to the first miraculous sign, they may believe the second. But if they do not believe these two signs . . . " (vv. 8-9). Then followed instructions that set the stage for the ten plagues. Moses performed the signs, and the people believed (4:30-31). The *signs* were miracles revealing the power of God to assure the people that it really was God who had sent Moses to deliver them. The *signs* and *wonders* that happened in Pharaoh's presence were intended to soften his heart and to warn him that God was deadly serious about his people's release. "Let my people go!" was not a casual suggestion for Pharaoh's meditation and reflection. It was a command to be obeyed. Disobedience would bring serious consequences. But Pharaoh grew more calloused until the last sign—death of the firstborn—hit even his own family. In the midst of grief, undoubtedly under great pressure, he weakened, only to change his mind a few days later.

One would think that the radical sign of hundreds of deaths, including that of one's own son, preceded by nine other miracles, would lead to instant, total conversion. Not so. Conversion itself is a miracle of God when the Spirit works in the human heart. A miracle may arouse questions, but unless the heart is open, the question is, "So what?" In one who has eyes to see and ears to hear, the miracle causes fear, awe, and trembling. But one who is blind or whose heart is hard can deny, explain, or resist that same miracle. The miracle, no matter how astonishing, may contribute to a conversion, but by itself it is inadequate. The converted are moved and touched, the unconverted become hardened or even cynical. The heart of Christianity lies in faith: "Anyone who comes to him must believe that he exists and that he rewards those who earnestly seek him" (Heb. 11:6).

In the Exodus story of Moses and Pharaoh, miracles were not limited to the power of the covenant-keeping God of Moses. When Moses and Aaron threw down the staff and it became a snake, the Egyptian magicians did the same thing (Ex. 7:11-12). When Moses' staff struck the water of the Nile, it turned to blood; the Egyptian magicians copied him (v. 22). It was the same for the plague of frogs (8:6), but when the magicians tried to copy the plague of gnats, they could not do it (v. 18). The magicians backed away after that. When the plague of boils came, "The magicians could not stand before Moses because of the boils that were on them and on all the Egyptians" (9:11). Again we see the conflict between the kingdom of God and Satan, but this time God says, "No gnats! This battle's mine!"

The plagues were miraculous signs to convince the Egyptians that the God of Israel was God. Instead of submitting in repentance, they hardened their hearts. The signs were also to benefit Israel, "that you may tell your children and grandchildren how I dealt harshly with the Egyptians and how I performed my signs among them, and that you may know that I am the LORD" (10:2).

Other Old Testament Miracles

Subsequent Old Testament passages referred back to the signs and wonders God performed before Pharaoh. In Deuteronomy 4, God reminded Israel about what their God had done and then added, "Has any god ever tried to take for himself one nation out of another nation, by testings, by miraculous signs and wonders . . . ? You were shown these things so that you might know that the LORD is God" (vv. 34-35). Moses repeated this reminder about God's miraculous signs and wonders in Deuteronomy 6:22 and 26:8. Moses also pointed the people ahead to the day when God would raise up a prophet like him from among their own (18:15), one who would do even greater signs and wonders.

The Old Testament miracles were *signs* perceived by the senses, and they served as a confirmation of the reality and presence of God. Rahab, in return for the kindness she had shown to the two spies, asked for kindness for her family and for a "sure sign" that their lives would be spared (Josh. 2:12-13). David prayed for "a sign of your goodness, that my enemies may see it and be put to shame" (Ps. 86:17).

Through the prophets, God called his people into acts of faith and obedience. In Isaiah 7, we read about King Ahaz, who was invited to ask God for a sign to confirm God's prophecy to him. Ahaz was rather reluctant, for he did not want to put God to the test. Then Isaiah, impatient with Ahaz, said, "Therefore the Lord himself will give you a sign: the virgin will be with child and will give birth to a son, and will call him Immanuel" (v. 14).

Signs were miracles God gave to prove to Old Testament people that he was the mighty one he claimed to be. For some, these mighty acts were signs of judgment. The plagues were warnings to Pharaoh but signs of God's power to the Israelites. The warnings became the enaction of judgment for the Egyptians when the Red Sea parted and swallowed them. The same sea became the place where God's people entered a new phase in their history. It became a place of praise and thanksgiving.

Miracles happened frequently during the days of Elijah, as recorded in 1 Kings 17-19. In fact, Elijah was involved in so many miracles that people concluded that he had reappeared when Christ performed miracles in the New Testament. Amazing demonstrations of God's power and care for his creation took place. We recall how the ravens brought Elijah bread and meat each day (1 Kings 17:4, 6), how the widow's "jar of flour was not used up and the jug of oil did not run dry" (v. 16), and how her son's "life returned to him, and he lived" (v. 22). Many miracles, like the one on Mount Carmel (18:16-45), were confrontations with other gods to show that Yahweh was the God of heaven and earth and the one worthy of honor.

As Elisha "picked up the cloak that had fallen from Elijah" to symbolize his succession, God demonstrated his power and presence by dividing the water of the Jordan (2 Kings 2:13-14). And then there are the stories many of us learned in church school: the widow's "little oil" that filled every jar she and her sons could gather (4:1-7), the Shunammite's son restored to life "mouth to mouth, eyes to eyes, hands to hands" (vv. 8-36), and Naaman healed of leprosy in spite of his temper-tantrum reaction to washing in the Jordan. Through a floating axhead (6:1-7) and blinded Aramean soldiers (vv. 8-23), God was demonstrating his concern for the Israelites and proving his power to their enemies.

It is clear that miracles abounded in certain periods of Old Testament times. They happened in nature as God formed the creation, released the flood, parted the Red Sea, made the sun stand still, dropped manna and quail from heaven, and created imbalances of nature (plagues) to confront Pharaoh. Others, sources of blessings and life, included healings and the raising of the dead. God provided bread from a jar of flour and supplied a jug of oil that kept pouring and pouring! Many of these miracles confirmed the reality of God; others were clear warnings of impending judgment. They were not be ignored or minimized; each one called for a response. Each proclaimed that God's kingdom had arrived and that it was coming. The writings of the prophets in particular prepared God's people for a "greater one" who would come. We meet this one, Jesus, in the New Testament.

Christ Healing the Blind

—Nicolas Poussin, 1594-1665

CHAPTER 5

MIRACLES AND THE MINISTRY OF JESUS

In defining the word *miracle* in Chapter 2, we observed that it was often used in the New Testament in various combinations with *signs* and *wonders* (see Acts 2:22, 43; 4:30; 5:12; 6:8; 7:36; 8:13; 14:3; and 15:12). Miracles were visible demonstrations of power, and the crowds who followed Jesus and his disciples wanted to know, "Who's behind this?" The miracles recorded in the four gospels were ascribed to Jesus, whom many, because of the miracles, viewed as the Messiah.

Empowered for Ministry

The New Testament introduced in person the Messiah who fulfilled Old Testament prophecies and expectations and performed many miracles. Before actively initiating his ministry, Jesus was declared to be God's beloved Son when the Spirit of God descended upon him as John baptized him in the Jordan (Matt. 3:13-17). Jesus was empowered to respond with perfect obedience to the Father's will and so truly became the second Adam. As a "filled-with-the-Spirit" human being, Jesus performed his ministry of teaching, preaching, and miracles. Thomas Smail, in his book *Reflected Glory,* beautifully describes the integration of the Trinity. He states that the fullness of the Holy Spirit present in the Lord Jesus Christ enabled him to live without sin, portray the power of God, and do miracles.

As we noted in Chapter 3, Jesus' miracles were directly related to the work of redemption for which he came. Jesus accompanied his signs and wonders with teaching that challenged the people to "turn from their wicked ways" in repentance. Religious rulers and leaders refused to acknowledge him as the Son of God. His miracles shouted at them, "Watch! If these are not the mighty works of God then how else are these things done?" But they refused to respond to Jesus. Instead, in their efforts to explain the miracles, they blasphemed by crediting power to Beelzebub, the prince of the kingdom of darkness (Mark 3:22). It was a serious sin to credit Satan and to refuse to acknowledge the power of God when God's "handwriting" was obvious. Without repentance, it was a sin unto death.

Besides declaring and demonstrating his identity, Jesus' healings showed the depth of his compassion: "When he saw the crowds, he had compassion on them . . . " (Matt. 9:36). Many of Jesus' healings brought relief from serious physical illnesses. Others attacked demons and involved exorcisms. In yet other instances, Jesus dealt with guilt and the need for forgiveness. His compassion led him to meet people's most pressing needs. Jesus loved people but hated the hurt and pain they were experiencing. He saw in those struggles the finger-prints of Satan combined with the consequences of our continued fall into sin. As part of his redemptive work, Jesus came to set the captives free, to heal, to raise to life, and to restore.

Miracles of Healing

A cursory reading of the gospels indicates that healing people was integral to Jesus' mission and ministry. In Mark's gospel, which is generally accepted as the main source for the writings of Matthew and Luke, nearly a third of the verses are about the miracles of Jesus. Morton Kelsey states that about "one-fifth of the entire gospels is devoted to Jesus' healing and discussions occasioned by it" (*Healing and Christianity*, p. 54). Kelsey's tally indicates that of 3,779 verses in the four gospels, 727 relate to the healing of physical and mental illnesses and to the resurrection of the dead. He counts another thirty-one general references to miracles that include healings. Forty-one stories in the gospels involve Jesus in the ministry of healing.

The gospel writers record no instance in which Jesus refused to heal some-one—*all* who came to Jesus for healing were healed. At times when healing was requested, forgiveness was granted—much to the chagrin of some bystanders who thought Jesus was out of line to declare forgiveness, because, in their minds, that was only the prerogative of God. It was no surprise that those who were healed went on their way skipping and dancing for joy, telling all who would listen what had happened to them. When religious leaders asked for pre-cise details and the sequence of events, one man, liberated from his prison of blindness, could only tell them, "One thing I do know. I was blind but now I see!" (John 9:25). He didn't know how it had happened, and it really didn't matter.

Although the healings had many similarities, Jesus treated each person uniquely. He didn't draw out nice formulas: "In case of leprosy, do . . . ; with deafness, the exact words are . . . ; and with blindness, use spit unless caused by. . . . " It simply was not that neat.

Jesus often touched people when they came to him and asked for healing. Luke says that "people brought to Jesus all who had various kinds of sickness, and laying his hands on each one, he healed them" (4:40). Mark reports that in his hometown Jesus couldn't do many miracles "except lay his hands on a few sick people and heal them" (6:5).

The gospel writers also record specific instances when Jesus initiated touch-ing. "A man with leprosy came to him and begged him on his knees, 'If you are willing, you can make me clean.' Filled with compassion, Jesus reached out his hand and touched the man . . . and he was cured" (Mark 1:40-42). Jesus laid his hands on a woman who had been bent over and deformed for eighteen years (Luke 13:13). He touched the eyes of two men who were blind, and their sight was restored (Matt. 9:29). In the Garden of Gethsemane, when Peter took it upon himself to defend his Lord by swinging a sword and cutting off Malchus's ear, Jesus touched the man's ear and healed him instantly (Luke 22:51).

Healings also occurred when a sick person touched Jesus. Matthew recalled, "People brought all their sick to him and begged him to let the sick just touch the edge of his cloak, and all who touched him were healed" (14:36). Obviously, many people were confident that Jesus could and would heal them. They knew enough about Jesus to warrant their following him. The woman who had been bleeding for twelve years dared a quick touch, hoping that she would benefit and that Jesus would never know: "Immediately her bleeding stopped and she . . . was freed from her suffering" (Mark 5:29). Jesus sensed the apparent drain of energy and praised the faith that led her to act.

In other cases there was no request, nor any touch, yet a person was healed. Mark 3:1-6 says Jesus was on his way into the temple when he noticed a man with a shriveled hand. The Pharisees closely watched to see if Jesus would heal on the Sabbath. Knowing their thoughts, Jesus asked, "Should one do good on the Sabbath or is that against the rules?" Jesus healed the man to show the Pharisees that he had the authority to reinterpret the sacred Sabbath laws.

Sometimes Jesus gave commands to bring about the healing. The man with the shriveled hand was told, "Stretch out your hand" (v. 5). The leper was ordered, "Be clean!" (1:41). To the man who couldn't walk, Jesus said, "Get up, take your mat and go home" (2:11). The ten lepers were told to go show themselves to the priest, and they were healed on the way (Luke 17:11-19). When Jesus healed the boy who was demon-possessed, "he rebuked the evil spirit. . . . 'Come out of him and never enter him again'" (Mark 9:25).

Some miraculous healings happened over distance. Matthew 8:5-13 tells about a centurion who came to Jesus to ask for help for his servant who "lies at home paralyzed and in terrible suffering" (v. 6). Jesus was willing to go to the man's home, but the centurion said, "Just say the word, and my servant will be healed" (v. 8). Jesus was "astonished" (v. 10) at the man's faith and healed the servant without going to him. A similar story is told in Matthew 15:21-28 about the Canaanite woman whose daughter's life was being destroyed by demons. Again, Jesus was impressed with the woman's faith and rewarded it by healing her daughter "from that very hour" (v. 28) without going to her house. These are two more examples of the relationship between faith and miracles, a topic we introduced in Chapter 2.

Miracles with Nature

Although the majority of the miracles that Jesus performed involved healings of various kinds, Christ also portrayed his authority and power over creation. Because only a few miracles involving nature are recorded in the gospels, most Christians are quite familiar with them.

At the beginning of Jesus' ministry, a wedding celebration about to collapse was allowed to continue when Christ changed water into wine (John 2:1-11). This was the first instance in which resources were multiplied, and it demonstrated that the kingdom of God is like a good wedding party at which the host provides all that is needed for a great celebration.

The multiplication of limited resources occurred again when Jesus fed five thousand men, plus a large number of women and children, with five loaves and two fishes (Mark 6:34-44). Jesus simply told the disciples to set the table for supper. Quite rationally, they responded, "We can't afford the grocery bill for so many! It will take eight months' salary to feed these guests." But Jesus took the resources available and divided the bread and fish "among them all" (v. 41). As the disciples distributed the bread and fish, it multiplied. Amazingly, they gathered up twelve baskets of leftovers, far more than what they had started with! This miracle beautifully revealed Jesus as the compassionate caretaker of people who were like "sheep without a shepherd" (v. 34). Jesus demonstrated that he was the provider of all their needs, the Lord whom all could follow and trust. Mark 8:1-9 describes a similar miracle when Jesus revealed his power and glory and fed four thousand people. Note that Mark reports this as a second, separate miracle; others consider it a second telling of the miracle recorded in Mark 6:34-44.

Matthew follows the story of the feeding of the five thousand with the miracle of walking on water (14:22-32). Jesus had sent out his disciples while he stayed behind to pray. When the wind picked up, the disciples fought the waves, trying to get back to land. Imagine their shock when they saw Jesus coming toward them, walking on water as though it had four inches (ten centimeters) of ice on it. Impetuous Peter asked to be allowed to "walk" to Jesus. He was invited and started out well; then Peter realized what he was doing and promptly sank. Jesus responded by telling Peter that doubts had overwhelmed his faith and had led him to sink; there was a direct relationship between faith, trust in Christ, and the ability to walk on water. Jesus showed his mastery *in* the storm by walking on the water and inviting and empowering Peter to do the same.

At another time, Jesus showed mastery *over* the storm by commanding it to be still. This story is recorded in the three synoptic gospels (Matt. 8:18, 23-27; Mark 4:35-41; Luke 8:22-25). While the disciples sailed across the sea, Jesus took a nap. The Sea of Galilee was known for winds and squalls that could arise unpredictably, quickly, and severely. A storm hit while the disciples were crossing, creating an ominous situation for the boat and its passengers. They were in danger of capsizing and drowning—unaware of their "life jacket" on board. Jesus continued to sleep, oblivious to the threat around him. Reluctantly the disciples woke him up and rebuked him for being indifferent to the fact that they might all drown. Jesus addressed the wind; it died down, the waves became calm, and the disciples were stunned. They asked, "Who is this? Even the wind and the waves obey him!" (Mark 4:41). Even creation was subordinate to the one whom the disciples were learning to call "master and Lord."

And fishing stories are not just twentieth-century phenomena—the disciples had some great ones. Challenged to pay their annual "church tithe" (Matt. 17:24-27), Peter was instructed to go fishing and was told that the first fish he would catch would have a coin in its mouth; he was to take it and pay the tax for himself and Jesus.

Peter had another story to top all fish stories (John 21:1-11). He, an accomplished, experienced fisherman, had been out all night. He was ready to go home skunked when a stranger on shore told him to throw his net out on the other side of the boat. Imagine Peter's thoughts: "We have been out all night trying. Who does he think he is?" But it was easier to comply than to question or argue. Imagine the shock and subsequent stories: 153 fish in one haul and torn nets to prove it! Through this post-resurrection miracle, the disciples recognized the stranger as the risen Jesus. And once again, Jesus provided for his disciples' needs and took Peter back! The power that showed that he was the Christ before Calvary continued to prove that he was the Son of God.

An incidental miracle involving nature is tucked away in the middle of another story. Upon leaving Bethany after the triumphal entry, Jesus came to a fig tree that had no figs on it (Mark 11:12-14, 20-25). He was hungry and had expected to eat its fruit, but it was not the season for fruit. Yet Jesus cursed the tree, and by the next morning it had withered. Jesus' surprised disciples were taught a principle about the importance of faith and prayer. If Jesus through faith and prayer could shrivel a fig tree, imagine what would happen if the disciples likewise had faith and were to speak to a mountain, ordering it to move and be cast into the sea: "Whatever you ask for in prayer, believe that you have received it, and it will be yours" (v. 24).

Some of the healing miracles, especially those involving demonic activity and exorcisms, can be explained rationally. The fish with money in its mouth? It could have found a coin that someone had lost. The coincidence would have been remarkable. The same for the great catch of fish. Likewise the stilling of the storm or Jesus' walking on water. The raising of the dead is often explained by suggesting that the person wasn't really dead but was unconscious or in a coma. But this explanation won't work in Lazarus's case, because the gospels record that he had been in the grave for three days. The transformation of water into wine and the multiplication of food and fish into vast meals for thousands defy natural explanations. They are miracles.

The Miracle of Miracles

Undoubtedly the miracle of all miracles was the resurrection of Jesus Christ. The fact of the resurrection is the foundation for the balance of the New Testament books. What one does with that story, recorded in all four gospels, determines one's relationship to Christ and the Christian faith. Indeed, our theology all flows from the miracle of Easter. If it did not happen, all subsequent hope based upon it collapses. As Paul says, "our preaching is useless" (1 Cor. 15:14) and "faith is futile" (v. 17). Life and hope for the entire Christian church are based on the reality of Christ's resurrection from the dead.

The resurrection, more clearly than any other miracle, calls for a response. It calls for a faith decision. It either happened, or it didn't. It can't be both or a little of each. When people are dead, they stay dead; if not, we believe they weren't really dead. Throughout history, many people have claimed that Jesus was not really dead. Theories abound to explain what happened, but the resurrection of Christ defies human explanation. When a man who is *truly* dead comes back to life, something supernatural has occurred. It can't be understood or explained precisely because it *is* a miracle; but because it has happened, all other miracles are easier to accept. The resurrection is that kind of a miracle. Miracles are the signs of Jesus Christ that point to his power and divinity; his resurrection is the apex of signs!

At the same time, once one reads the history of redemption, it is most natural for Christ to be raised from the dead. Once sin is destroyed, the consequence of sin—death—has also lost its power. Thus the resurrection of Jesus could have been expected as a most natural result of and a conclusion to his redemptive work. And for the new creation to come, when sin and Satan have lost their hold on the human race, resurrections will be the "natural" event of the day.

The New Testament revealed Jesus as the son of God. This was done through his life and his ministry but particularly through his death and resurrection. That was and is today the crux of the Christian faith. It is not the other way around. It is not that miracles convince us that Jesus is the Christ, the Savior, and because of them we entrust him with our lives. Rather, as the Son of God, Jesus has restored our relationship to the Father. Once we openly acknowledge and confess that belief, miracles simply confirm and deepen our faith.

I first met Abebe and Kelemua Mengistu soon after they moved into the neighborhood near Oakdale Park Christian Reformed Church. They were newly married immigrants from Ethiopia and occasionally attended worship services at the church.

The couple rejoiced when Kelemua became pregnant. From time to time they met with members of the church who encouraged them as they prepared for their child's birth. In September 1998, Abraham came into the world suddenly under traumatic circumstances, when two months before her due date Kelemua was in an automobile accident and went into labor. Abraham was born with many of the problems of a premature birth and in addition had a blood clot on his brain due to the automobile accident.

As a congregation, we began to pray for Abraham, who was receiving excellent care in the neonatal unit at Spectrum Hospital in Grand Rapids, Michigan. Slowly he began to grow, but the blood clot continued to threaten his life. After numerous tests, the doctors determined his best hope for survival was a delicate brain surgery that carried great risk of complications that could cause life-long disabilities.

The Monday before the surgery was scheduled, Abebe, Kelemua, Edith Bajema (a member of Oakdale's prayer team), and I joined in prayer around Abraham's incubator. I remember how my heart was moved at the sight of Abebe and Kelemua, new parents in a new country, in a new language with a new faith, kneeling in prayer and pleading with God for the life of their son. Early the next morning, as the doctors conducted their tests before surgery, they discovered that God had worked a miracle overnight. Abraham's blood clot was gone! Not only did the doctors cancel surgery, but that very day they determined that Abraham was healthy enough to go home.

Since then, Abraham has grown to be an alert, smiling child, and further checkups have cleared him of all the medical problems related to his birth. Abebe and Kelemua have made profession of their faith in Jesus Christ, and the whole family has been welcomed into God's family at Oakdale Park Church.

—William VandenBosch.
Used by permission of Abebe and Kelemua Mengistu.

William VandenBosch is pastor of Oakdale Park Christian Reformed Church, an inner-city congregation of about four hundred members in Grand Rapids, Michigan.

Christ's dialogue with the Pharisees in Matthew 12:38-45 confirmed that reality. They asked him for a "miraculous sign" (v. 39). Jesus said he did not give signs for curiosity or for the sake of convincing someone. But he also said that one sign, like the sign of Jonah, would be given: "the Son of Man will be three days and three nights in the heart of the earth" (v. 40), an obvious reference to his burial and resurrection. Jesus gave the same answer in John 2:18-23 when the Jews demanded a sign. Jesus said, "'Destroy this temple, and I will raise it again in three days'" (v. 19). Later the disciples recognized that Jesus was speaking of his body and the resurrection to come. The Pharisees later saw that sign fulfilled but did not believe.

Some people are still not convinced even today. While on a tour in Israel, we were led by a Jewish guide as we "ran where Jesus walked." For a week our guide showed us the significant places in the life of Jesus. He knew thoroughly the history of the area and the New Testament and spoke openly about the many events in the life of Jesus. Toward the end of the week, after having seen the place of the skull and the possible places of the tomb, I asked our guide what he thought occurred on that Easter Sunday morning. I was shocked by his response: "I have no doubt that Jesus arose from the dead. I and many others of my people have no other explanation for the subsequent changes that took place after that event." But that had not convinced him that Jesus was the long-awaited Messiah. He and thousands of others are still waiting and watching.

Through the work of the Spirit, the church is a strong witness and testimony to the miracle of the resurrection. In the next chapter we will look at the impact of that miracle on the early church.

The Healing of the Cripple - Detail #1 (from The Life of St. Peter cycle)   —Masaccio, 1401-ca. 1428

CHAPTER 6

MIRACLES IN THE EARLY CHURCH

Although this chapter will focus on miracles that occurred during the days of the early Christian church, we should note that the disciples completed a "miracle apprenticeship" while Jesus was on earth. Mark tells us that Jesus "sent them out two by two and gave them authority over evil spirits. . . . They drove out many demons and anointed sick people with oil and healed them" (6:6, 13). Further empowered by the Holy Spirit at Pentecost, the apostles continued to perform miracles to demonstrate God's love and power and to carry on the work of Christ, their great Teacher and master miracle worker. We'll see proof of the Spirit's work as we take a broad sweep through the book of Acts, noting especially Peter's bold preaching and miracles, and then we'll look specifically at Paul's ministry.

The Work of the Apostles

The Scriptures clearly indicate that miracles continued to occur after Jesus ascended. When Christ ended his earthly ministry, he continued his kingly work from the perspective of the Father's right hand. Jesus told his disciples to wait for the Holy Spirit, who would equip them to continue the work of Christ on earth (Acts 1:4, 7).

Pentecost made prophets out of all of God's people. Moses' longing—"I wish that all the LORD's people were prophets and that the LORD would put his Spirit on them!"—was fulfilled (Num. 11:29). The event was accompanied by the miracle of tongues in which the "wonders of God" (Acts 2:11) were declared in various languages. Three thousand new "births" took place in response to Peter's preaching. The miraculous outpouring of God's Spirit resulted in conversions and changed lives (vv. 42-47), which in turn led to more conversions as "the Lord added to their number daily those who were being saved" (v. 47). It was a marvelous time in the history of the church!

Luke follows the story of Pentecost with the account of Peter and John on the way to the temple. When a man crippled from birth begged them for money, Peter ordered him to get up and walk, and the man did! Peter, before an astonished and hushed crowd that saw him as a hero, explained that the credit for healing the beggar who couldn't walk did not belong to him. "Men of Israel, why does this surprise you? Why do you stare at us as if by our own power or godliness we had made this man walk?" (Acts 3:12). The glory went to God. Peter made it plain that the important point here was not the miracle of healing but the call to repentance, and he invited the crowd to place their faith in Jesus, the one whom they had crucified.

The apostles' faith, along with their spiritual empowerment, gave them the courage to act and preach fearlessly. All of it seemed miraculous to onlookers, who wondered out loud, "What happened to these guys?" They were the same people who had shrunk back with fear when Jesus' life had been threatened only a few weeks earlier. The crowds recognized that these men had been with Jesus and that their message was real (Acts 4:13). Through miracles and healings, the apostles made it clear that, though they were the agents, the work was that of Christ; it was accomplished through faith in him. They were in touch with God, who confirmed his Word and "accredited" his Son to the people by "miracles, wonders, and signs" (2:22). The apostles continued similar work to demonstrate that the call to repent and turn to Christ was important and urgent.

The outpouring or the filling of the Holy Spirit is repeatedly mentioned in the book of Acts. Where this happened, changes resulted. In Acts 2, people who were filled with the Spirit spoke in tongues, and thousands of conversions took place. In Acts 4:5-12 we see that Peter, filled with the Spirit, had a new boldness to testify that the man who couldn't walk was healed in the name of Jesus. And he testified in front of rulers and elders who were determined to put him away! Two months earlier Peter had been scared to admit to a young girl that he was with Christ; now he was risking his life for the same Master. He was a changed man! With the believers, Peter and John prayed that threats on their lives would not result in compromise but that they would speak "with great boldness" (v. 29). They wanted courage to represent the Christ who was using their hands to "heal and perform miraculous signs and wonders" (v. 30). As a result, "they were all filled with the Holy Spirit and spoke the word of God boldly" (v. 31).

For the apostles, the filling of the Holy Spirit was frequently accompanied by miracles. In Acts 5:1-11, Peter exercised radical church discipline because he had been given miraculous knowledge about the lies of Ananias and Sapphira. The apostles performed "many miraculous signs and wonders among the people" (v. 12), and "more and more men and women believed" (v. 14). As a result, crowds from the areas around Jerusalem brought the sick for healing and the demonized for exorcism; some just wanted Peter's shadow to fall on them. Luke, the physician, reported that "all of them were healed" (v. 16).

When Peter visited Lydda, Aeneas, a paralytic who had been bedridden for eight years, was healed (9:32-35). "All those who lived in Lydda and Sharon saw him and turned to the Lord" (v. 35). Luke reported that Peter prayed for Dorcas, who had died and was mourned deeply by her friends (vv. 36-43). Peter ordered Dorcas to get up, and she did! Word of that miracle spread all over

Joppa, "and many people believed in the Lord" (9:42). Miracles repeatedly resulted in people being converted and changed.

The believers witnessed miracles other than healings. Acts 12:1-19 tells how Peter—in prison and about to be killed—was unchained by an angel while the church "was earnestly praying" (v. 5). When God released him and Peter knocked on the door to join the praying church, they refused to believe the news that God had actually answered their prayers and had granted Peter release from prison. But when they saw him "they were astonished" (v. 16).

The inevitable was bound to happen. The evil one did not lie dormant when God was majestically at work, revealing his power and glory. The more radically the gospel was preached and the more boldly it was demonstrated with miracles, the more certain its opposition. The apostles were given "strict orders not to teach in this name" (5:27), but they could not stop. That would have been disobedient to God, and they had no intention of dishonoring him—again! They were flogged and ordered to keep quiet about Jesus (v. 40), but they did not. Instead, they rejoiced in the persecution that came their way. They made an impact for Christ because their witness was so obviously offensive to the religious leaders. To suffer disgrace for Christ's sake was a badge of honor (5:41).

It was not uncommon for Christians to be flogged as the apostles were. Simon Kistemaker, in *The New Testament Commentary, Acts* (p. 213) explains this punishment:

> According to the Mosaic Law, a man who is guilty of a crime deserves to receive a beating. The judge orders the man to lie down in his presence. He punishes the man with the number of lashes he has decreed, but he may not exceed forty lashes (Deut. 25:2-3). The flogging was administered with a calfskin whip on the bare upper part of the body.

New Testament persecution continued with Stephen's stoning (7:54-60), a cruel, dreadful way to die, "but Stephen, full of the Holy Spirit, looked up to heaven and saw the glory of God, and Jesus standing at the right hand of God" (v. 55). "A great persecution broke out against the church" (8:1) the day Stephen was martyred. The believers were scattered, and "Saul began to destroy the church" (v. 3).

Yet through it all, the Holy Spirit gave the apostles the power to perform miracles, enabled them to give bold testimony to the risen Lord, and gave them miraculous courage to die with the glory of Jesus on their faces in spite of ugly, vicious persecution. Even Saul, who first persecuted the church, could not escape the power of the Spirit. Who would have imagined that one who "was there, giving approval to [Stephen's] death" (v. 1), would someday testify, "I have . . . been in prison more frequently, been flogged more severely . . . five times I received from the Jews the forty lashes minus one . . . once I was stoned . . . so that Christ's power may rest on me" (2 Cor. 11:23-25; 12:9).

The Ministry of Paul

Acts 9 begins with a radical conversion: Saul, the persecutor and perpetrator of evil against the Christian church, becomes Paul, a missionary to the Gentiles. Paul's conversion was a powerful demonstration of what the Holy Spirit does when he grabs hold of a person. God first confronted Paul with two miracles: blindness, and then restoration of sight as Ananias laid hands on him. Then, like Peter, Paul was empowered by God to preach the word and to continue the work of Jesus. He was "set apart" (13:2) with Barnabas, ordained with prayer and the laying on of hands, and commissioned as a missionary.

On their very first journey, Paul and Barnabas met Elymas the sorcerer (13:8). Paul dealt with Elymas's deceit and trickery by pronouncing blindness upon him (v. 11). The miracle was a confrontation between the power of God and the evil one, and God was obviously the more powerful one. Note again, as we did with the ten plagues in the Old Testament, that not all miracles are beneficial to those who are affected by them. Elymas's blindness, as well as the deaths of Ananias and Sapphira, were awesome evidence that the gospel message is to be carefully heard and seriously obeyed.

Ministry and miracles often occurred together in Paul's life, and the combination brought him trouble and persecution. In Lystra, Paul met a man who had such crippled feet that he had never walked in his life (14:8-10). Paul noted his faith and ordered the man to stand up on his useless feet, and he did. In Acts 16:16-24, we're told that a young woman, controlled by a spirit that predicted the future, followed Paul and his group around for days and harassed them. Finally Paul had had enough and ordered the spirit to come out. It did. The "pimps" who were making big money on the woman's fortune-telling were distressed by their loss of a source of income, so they took Paul and Silas into court. The two were stripped and beaten, severely flogged, and thrown into prison with their feet fastened in the stocks. Their midnight escape from prison, and the subsequent conversion of the jailer, was another miracle (vv. 25-34).

In Troas, Paul's long sermon led Eutychus to fall "into a deep sleep as Paul talked on and on" (20:9). Sound asleep, Eutychus fell out of the third floor window "and was picked up dead." Paul threw himself on the young man, and he was brought back to life. A similar death-defying miracle occurred when a snake latched its fangs into Paul's hand (28:1-6). Those who saw it expected the arm to swell and Paul to drop dead. Because he did not do so, they called him a god. While visiting Publius, the chief official of the island, Paul learned that Publius's father "was sick in bed, suffering from fever and dysentery" (v. 8). Paul prayed, laid hands on him, and he was healed. After that, word of Paul's miracles got around and "the rest of the sick on the island came and were cured" (v. 9).

Throughout the book of Acts, Luke reports that miracles were a part of Paul's ministry. On seven occasions he reports multiple miracles, three involving Paul. As a consequence, "The whole assembly became silent as they listened to Barnabas and Paul telling about the miraculous signs and wonders God had done among the Gentiles through them" (15:12). As a casual aside, Luke mentions that "God did extraordinary miracles through Paul, so that even handkerchiefs and aprons that had touched him were taken to the sick, and their illnesses were cured and the evil spirits left them" (19:11-12). God used Paul, and, as easily as he used people, God likewise could use items. God was the one who was consistently the healer; the agents used varied widely.

Miracles created fear and admiration in Paul's day, just as they do now (see Acts 19:11-20), but they never became the primary focus of Paul's ministry. His ministry focused on taking the gospel to a Gentile world. The message stood by itself. Miracles were demonstrations that authenticated the message's impact; they were *incidental, not primary* to the ministry. Paul's success in healing and exorcism did not cause him to become a celebrity who hit the road with income-producing miracle crusades. Neither did the presence or absence of miracles affect his journeys. Following the example of Jesus, no matter how many people were being healed and set free, Paul moved on when the time came. Instead of prolonging "miracle services" that were going well in Ephesus, Paul decided to go to Jerusalem, after which he had to get to Rome.

Paul's message, like Peter's, was redemption through repentance and faith in Jesus Christ. That was first and foremost. It was the driving force of his ministry and mission. All other things were subservient. Paul preached that Christ had been crucified and was raised from the dead. He was willing to give his life for Christ and to preach the message of grace. The time would come when that horrible option became reality. Paul said, "For to me, to live is Christ and to die is gain" (Phil. 1:21). Paul's outlook on life was one in which he could not lose. The worst persecution could do to him would be to snuff out his life. To others that would appear to be a terrible defeat, but for Paul it would be victory. It's all a matter of one's perspective on life. It's the hope of the resurrection miracle.

The Raising of Lazarus

—Tot Sint Jans Geertgen, 1457-1485

DO MIRACLES OCCUR TODAY?

Miracles were common events in New Testament writings, as we saw in the previous chapter. But the big question for many Christians is whether miracles happen *today.* And do miracles occur only in Christian circles? If so, we can associate miracles with the existence of God, exclude them from other religions, and thus prove the reliability of the Christian faith. Not so simple!

Not Limited to Christianity

The Judeo-Christian world accepted miracles as a natural part of life. They expected them and prayed for them. The *Theological Dictionary of the New Testament,* Volume II (p. 302) states that

> the Hellenistic and Jewish world is full of miracles, happenings and gods and miracle workers. The miracles of Jesus are distinguished in three ways from others of that period:
>
> - The New Testament miracles of Jesus have no connection with magic, or with magic means and processes like the majority of miracles outside of the New Testament. . . .
>
> - The miracles are evoked by the powerful Word of Jesus, which has nothing to do with magic. On the contrary, he provokes defensive magic against himself which he overcomes with his Word of power. . . .
>
> - The miracles presuppose faith in the One who performs them and also of the one on who they are performed. We noted in earlier chapters that this was not always the case in Jesus' ministry.

In *That You May Believe* (p. 11), Colin Brown notes that John Calvin also distinguished between miracles that honor God and those that do not:

> Quoting John 7:18 and 8:50, Calvin pointed out that true miracles bring glory to God. They have no other purpose than to glorify the name of God. But there are also Satanic signs and wonders that deceive those who refuse to love the truth (2 Thess. 2:9-10). There are signs and wonders performed by false prophets who seek to lead people astray after other gods (Deut. 13). In short, the miraculous

on its own was not for Calvin sufficient proof of God's activity. The true test of a miracle was whether it brought glory to God.

A few centuries later, Abraham Kuyper (1837-1920) wrote an extensive, three-volume theological work in part of which he discussed miracles. Jan Boer, a Christian Reformed missionary in Nigeria, has summarized some of Kuyper's thoughts:

> Another intriguing aspect of Kuyper's view on miracles is his empha-
> sis on the fact that the power to perform miracles has been retained
> by various practitioners of traditional and Muslim religions. While
> today's Christians tend to deny followers of other religions that
> power and often relegate it to the world of tricks and deceit, Kuyper
> points to the Egyptian wise men of Moses' days as well as to the plain
> and undeniable reports of such powers brought to his attention by
> returned missionaries. It is time modern Christians once again
> acknowledge these powers.
>
> —Abraham Kuyper, *You Can Do Greater Things Than Christ*, p. 4.

Though miracles were very much a part of the ancient world, the renaissance and enlightenment, along with the reformation, elevated rational thought and the scientific method. It was not respectable for scholarly people to be unable to explain unique events that were at least unnatural if not miraculous. Thus explanations abounded, arguments ensued, debates raged, and miracles seemingly decreased as discussions increased. We'll explore some of the debate about whether miracles still occur today.

Did Miracles Occur During the Early
Centuries of the Christian Church?

As we noted in the previous chapter, the miraculous work of Christ continued after his ascension. The book of Acts describes a variety of miraculous demonstrations, most of them bringing healing from illnesses or long-standing disabilities and freedom from evil spirits and their bondages. But did they continue after the closing of the Canon of Scripture? Theologians vary radically in their responses. Some firmly respond, "Yes, miracles are common today and can be expected at any time in the life of the church." Others adamantly say, "Absolutely not. With the closing of the Canon of Scripture, we have the full revelation of God's Word and no longer need miracles to verify the reality of God and the veracity of the Messiah."

Did healings continue to occur in the centuries after the founding of the Christian church? Bernard Martin, pastor of the Reformed Church in Geneva, believes they did. In his book *The Healing Ministry in the Church* (p. 36), Martin writes,

> A study of the first three centuries of the Christian church shows clearly that the healing ministry of the church was practiced in the course of her history but that, gradually, its importance waned. It did not, however, completely disappear. If, at certain times, one can hardly find traces of it, the fact remains that at all times throughout the history of the Church miracles of healing were accomplished and have thus established a continuity from the beginning until our own times.

Martin finds support for his beliefs in the writings of some of the early church fathers. Irenaeus (A.D. 180) wrote, "There are acts of healing that only Christians are capable of accomplishing." Irenaeus indicated that the ministries of healing continued as prayer and the laying on of hands were practiced. Origen (A.D. 250) wrote, "There are still preserved among Christians traces of that Holy Spirit which . . . expel evil spirits, and perform many cures, and foresee certain events. . . . The name of Jesus can still remove distractions from the minds of men, and expel demons, and also take away diseases." Martin notes, "Even in the works of Augustine in the fifth century we find that he mentions many miracles which he witnessed himself."

In his book *Healing: Reflections on the Gospel,* George Martin writes that Augustine recorded seventy miracles in two years in the Diocese of Hippo (p. 28). A thousand years later in 1545, Luther, when asked what to do for a man who was mentally ill, wrote instructions for a healing service. It included a prayer for healing in Christ's name. Luther also saw his own friend Melanchthon brought back from the point of death through his prayers (Kelsey, *Healing and Christianity,* p. 233).

Today? No

Despite the evidence that miracles continued to occur during the early centuries of the Christian church, strong voices state that miracles and supernatural gifts ceased after the closing of the New Testament era. The reformers were not all in agreement with Martin Luther's position. Calvin certainly wasn't, as this statement indicates: "But the gift of healing, like the rest of the miracles, which the Lord willed to be brought forth for a time, has vanished away in order to make the new preaching of the gospel marvelous forever (*Institutes of the Christian Religion, The Library of Christian Classics,* Vol. XXI, p. 1467).

Calvin states this even more strongly as he combats the Roman Catholic sacrament of Extreme Unction, which is based on James 5:16. Though he denies the gift of healing, Calvin does emphasize the very presence of God at all times (p. 1467):

> Therefore, they make themselves ridiculous when they boast that they are endowed with the gift of healing. The Lord is indeed present with his people in every age; and he heals their weaknesses as often as necessary, no less than of old; still he does not put forth these manifest powers, nor dispense miracles through the apostles' hands. For that was a temporary gift, and also quickly perished partly on account of men's ungratefulness.

Others support Calvin in this debate. Benjamin B. Warfield, in a book ironically titled *Miracles: Yesterday and Today,* is strongly committed to the view that miracles ceased with the apostles (pp. 5-6). His comments are clear:

> How long did this state of things continue? It was the characterizing peculiarity of specifically the Apostolic Church, and it belonged therefore exclusively to the Apostolic age—although no doubt this designation may be taken with some latitude. These gifts were not the possession of the primitive Christian as such; nor for that matter of the Apostolic Church or the Apostolic age for themselves; they were distinctively the authentication of the apostles. They were part of the credentials of the apostles as the authoritative agents of God in the founding of the Church. Their function thus confined them to distinctively the Apostolic Church, and they necessarily passed away with it.

Reiterating his position, Warfield makes this argument (p. 9):

> This, then, is the theory: that, miracles having been given for the purpose of founding the church, they continued so long as they were needed for that purpose; growing gradually fewer as they were less needed, and ceasing altogether when the church having, so to speak, been firmly put upon its feet, was able to stand on its own legs.

Variations of Warfield's position remain with the church today. However, the effect of charismatic renewal has touched many evangelical and Roman Catholic churches that for many decades—even centuries, in some cases—accepted that miracles no longer occurred in the church today. Many of them were jolted when healings occurred within their congregations. My own denomination, the Christian Reformed Church, was among them. In 1973, the denomination officially changed its position to state that there is no biblical reason why spiritual gifts should be limited to the apostolic era—that they could appear at any time during any era.

Today? Yes

The issue has astute theologians supporting each side through different periods of church history. Usually, the closing of the Canon of Scripture is used as the reason for no longer experiencing the miraculous. At the same time, we hear amazing stories about events and healings for which there are no other explanations unless they are miracles. The same debate raged regarding spiritual gifts. Before the charismatic movement of the 1970s surfaced, spiritual gifts such as tongues, interpretations, prophecies, and miracles were common only in churches of Pentecostal affiliation. No respectable evangelical or Reformed congregation would tolerate such "spurious gifts" and "divisive" activities. In fact, the church's respectability was at stake if it admitted it tolerated "tongue-speaking Christians." Tremendous church battles and splits occurred over spiritual gifts.

However, evangelical and Reformed denominations were faced with the fact that some of their fine, respectable members had discovered one or more of these "spurious" gifts. Healings of various kinds happened in their congregations. It was hard to deny the reality of God portrayed in these revitalized Christians. Many of their lives had changed. Though some church leaders were impatient with and intolerant of these new challenges, others, over a period of time, genuinely began to accept gifted Christians who also met the tests of bearing fruit. Many churches learned what Dutch theologian G. C. Berkouwer so poignantly stated in *The Providence of God* (pp. 241-242):

> Thus God, even after the establishment of salvation in Christ, will go his way and build the Church through signs and miracles. And we find nothing in the Scriptures to indicate a line that we can draw through a definite period to mark off a boundary between the time of the absence of miracles. . . . The many signs that still appear after Pentecost should make us the more careful not to set limits, in our enlightened era, to the miraculous activity of God. There is not a single datum in the New Testament which makes it certain that God, in a period of strengthening and extending of the church in heathendom, will not confirm his message with signs, in holy resistance to the demonic influences of the kingdom of darkness. He who thinks that he can say with certainty that miracles no longer can occur may seriously ask himself whether he thinks in terms of God's power over the world or from a secret capitulation to determinism.

This is a very strong statement warranting some reflection. It comes from a respectable Reformed theologian who, in an academic setting, categorically states that there is no New Testament text that indicates that spiritual gifts or miracles are relegated to certain eras and not to others. Various conclusions may be drawn based upon one's experience, one's reading of history, or even one's theology. Academicians tend to be skeptical of anything subjective, personal, and unexplainable like signs and miracles. However, for those who are Reformed, the confession *sola scriptura* (only the Scriptures) dictates that only the Scriptures have the authoritative standing to give the final word. And as Berkouwer says, like it or not, the Bible gives no datum anywhere that indicates that God will not move with "signs and wonders" in any era for the purpose of extending the church. The Spirit moves when and where it wills; at the same time the Spirit's power is realized most evidently where there is a willingness and openness to the life of the Spirit. Because God is patient and gentle, God does not impose this power unwillingly upon us but comes gladly when we cordially invite the Spirit.

As we were reminded in chapter 5, Jesus was empowered by the Holy Spirit for ministry, and we are commanded to be filled with the Spirit (Eph. 5:18) as Jesus was. Because of Christ's death and resurrection and through similar empowerment by the Spirit, we continue Christ's work and "do even greater things" than Jesus did (John 14:12). To be filled comes to us as a command even though it is an action in which we are passive; God does the filling. Paul explains how God does this in the parallel passage of Colossians 3:16 when he calls us to "let the word of Christ dwell in you richly. . . ." In the New Testament church, the obedience of yielding to Word and Spirit was often accompanied by signs and wonders that confirmed God's word for his struggling children and extended God's church and kingdom. If that is still God's goal, should we be surprised when miracles occur?

If all that happens today through the mighty, ongoing work of the Spirit of God, why is it so hard for the church today to acknowledge that God performs other miracles? Do we quench (1 Thess. 5:19) or "resist" (Acts 7:51) the Spirit and unconsciously deny that miracles occur? Are we consciously, rigidly closed to the fresh life the Holy Spirit gives when God's people receive power and gifts?

The very same Spirit who moved through the life and ministry of Christ desires to move through the lives and ministries of his people today. Paul commands Christians to "be filled with Spirit" (Eph. 5:18). This is an ongoing, day-by-day process in which the Holy Spirit gives us the power to grow in grace, love, and holiness. So miracles today should not surprise us. In *You Can Do Greater Things Than Christ,* Abraham Kuyper makes quite a point of the fact that miracles are part of the Spirit-filled life and are not unique to Christ. The fullness of the Spirit enabled Christ's humanity to take control of nature again, as before the fall. A humanity redeemed and restored by the work of the Holy Spirit will have the ability to perform miracles as a natural outflow of that restoration.

Our Western Worldview

Our Western worldview is a major obstacle. We do not expect miracles. Our respect for the rational, scientific, and empirical creates mental blocks. We place great trust in our senses. If we cannot touch it, see it, feel it, hear it, smell it, or taste it, its existence is questionable.

Some years ago I was attending a large healing service in California. The star that night was Kathryn Kuhlman. My critical faculties, nurtured at schools and university, were well tuned and ready for action. Frankly I was not expecting anything to happen. I was finding it a struggle not to reject the whole affair as superficial showmanship, a vulgar form of show biz transferred from the secular to the Christian stage. Suddenly Kathryn announced to a crowd of several thousand people that God was healing a young man of emphysema. His lungs had been seriously damaged when he had been involved in a fire. About forty yards from where I was sitting a young man sprang to his feet and went quickly up to the platform. He was beaming from ear to ear. "You are healed," Kathryn said, and the young man obviously believed her. "Run down to the end of the auditorium and back," she commanded. This he proceeded to do, to the ecstatic delight of the audience. They cheered him all the way. By this time I was ready to write the whole thing off. It had clearly been rigged. The young man was an exhibitionist. He had not really been ill at all. It had been a case of mistaken identity. The cure was psychologically induced. Kathryn Kuhlman knew this young man and his case history. These were some of the possibilities which came into my mind. But a miracle—certainly not. Every kind of rational explanation bounced backwards and forwards in my brain. The possibility that we had witnessed a miracle never occurred to me.

I turned instinctively to the man sitting next to me who was a complete stranger. I asked him what he thought about it all, with a bit of a sarcastic edge to my voice. I immediately noticed that he had been deeply moved, and I was soon to know why. "That is my boy," he said. I was taken aback. I asked him several questions, and he told me the whole story. His son had been told by the doctors that his lungs had been so badly damaged he would never be able to run again. Prior to that evening he had been unable to walk more than fifty yards without severe breathlessness. No, he was not known to Kathryn Kuhlman, who had no prior knowledge of his condition. I learned a lesson that evening never to limit God and never to judge people or situations by outward impressions alone.

—Michael Harper, *The Healings of Jesus*, p. 13.

In our sophisticated Western church, miracles are not a routine part of our spirituality. Congregational experiences simply have not included interruptions or interferences from the miraculous. Spiritual gifts are looked upon as talents. Many respectable evangelical and Reformed Christians readily sing, "He touched me . . . It took a miracle to make me whole." But they become cautious, evasive, and general when asked to explain how God touched them. I have been in groups of leaders where these issues were discussed and where some participants spoke condescendingly about what they viewed as frivolous, frenzied activity. I have cringed in such conversations. At times I have raised enough courage to challenge or question the rather harsh judgments; at other times, I have kept quiet, not wanting to be seen as "one of those weird ones." Later I would confess to God for being a coward who was too concerned with his own image in front of others, especially colleagues.

Charismatic renewal led to major changes in the church. A growing hunger for greater spiritual vitality and power led many Christians to search beyond their own churches. Sometimes this was done with the knowledge—but rarely with the blessing—of their leaders. More often small groups would sneak a visit to "miracle services" that brought them into contact with Pentecostal Christians who previously had been viewed as rather foreign. Loyal church members who were in a desperate search for healing and who had already been prayed for in their own congregations crossed radical denominational boundaries to attend revival services. Leaders criticized and ridiculed Kathryn Kuhlman, even from their pulpits, while some of their members quietly scanned newspapers to see if she was going to be anywhere within five hundred miles of where they lived. If she was, they were going, with or without the knowledge or blessing of their church. Some came back healed; others did not. For those who went, the issue was simple: healing for some is better than no healing for all!

At about the same time, missionaries who were returning for furloughs from various third-world countries were testifying to the miraculous power of God overseas. This added to the shift in our Western churches. Charles Kraft describes the situation in his book *Christianity with Power* (p. xii):

> In order to understand and appropriate New Testament power, though, we have had to fight a formidable enemy. The cultural conditioning passed on to us through our family, school, and church has not been conducive to understanding and following our Master and his early followers in the area of spiritual power.

Kraft, like many other missionaries, discovered his own spiritual powerlessness when he served as a missionary in Nigeria. He was unprepared to deal with the Nigerians' spirit world. They specifically identified diseases, accidents, infertility, drought, and other disasters as the work of evil beings. And though Christians claimed that the power of God could heal and deliver from the demons, "we never demonstrated what we claimed in this area" (pp. 3-5). Kraft states that, though many Nigerians became Christians, they did not expect any healing power from Christianity, only help in medicine, education, and agriculture. They developed a "a loyalty to Christianity to handle certain needs paralleled by a continuing loyalty to traditional religious practitioners to handle their power needs. As missionaries we decried this practice, but we had no antidote" (p. 4).

These African Christians clearly saw the battles of the spirit world. Our Western view has tended to develop a duality: God forgives the sins of his people, and the medical people heal their diseases. God is often left as a last resort to be called on only when other techniques are unsuccessful.

Our attitude toward so-called "Pentecostal experiences" and spiritual gifts has softened. Testimonies of miracles are now regularly shared in many congregations. Books and articles appear in conservative churches encouraging all to have open hearts to what God might well be doing. Fear and skepticism have turned to cautious participation. For many, harsh, judgmental criticism has softened.

The opposite is also true. Some leaders have drawn clear lines to mark off their turf, urging and sometimes ordering their people to stay away from any and all charismatic activity. They declare tongue speaking and the like to be demonic, divisive, and destructive. In their view, these things are not a part of the true church today. Many members docilely follow their leaders' counsel as long as they experience physical and spiritual stability. But the door cracks open when in a time of struggle they find their own church unable to meet their needs, or when friends who attend another church visit with them and glowingly tell them about their experiences. The glue that has traditionally created loyalty to one's own church is no longer holding. The practice of worshiping or fellowshiping with congregations other than one's own has become common and quite acceptable. Most pastors have become aware that they are competing with other congregations and denominations for their members' loyalty.

Spiritual gifts and miracles, which usually come together, are now common in most denominations. Increased emphasis upon the matter of prayer is also bringing major changes into many denominations. Part of the change is a greater openness to praying for healing. In cases of crisis and emergency, prayer was always present; virtually every congregation has stories of how God healed certain people in their church. Now more churches are seeking, praying, and expecting God to respond, even miraculously. Amazingly, God does!

The Sick Child   —Edvard Munch, 1863-1944

CHAPTER 8

WHEN GOD DOES NOT HEAL

Why doesn't God heal everyone who asks for it? Frankly, for those who flagrantly dishonor or ignore God's revealed will, suffering is, at least partially, their own fault. We see others who have brought pain upon themselves as a result of years of self-abuse. But why does a loving God continue to allow pain and suffering in situations like these:

- A young child who, while enthusiastically enjoying life, becomes sick with leukemia. Over a period of time every vestige of life is painfully stripped from that tender little body and every ounce of energy from the child's parents.

- A twenty-eight-year-old godly, gifted pastor dies in an accident, leaving behind a distraught young mother with three preschoolers and a deeply wounded, confused congregation.

- A dedicated teacher fights a losing battle with cancer in spite of the prayers of her fifth-grade students and a host of God's family across the country.

Why all this pain, suffering, and death? It makes no sense. Couldn't our loving God have prevented the pain and suffering or healed by a miracle?

Our culture today sees pain and suffering as totally negative and to be avoided at all costs. Because they seem to have no beneficial value whatsoever, the "why" questions arise with great frequency. "If God is a loving God, why so much pain and grief?" we challenge. The biblical view of pain and God's involvement with our pain and grief is different. Knowing the benefits of pain makes the absence of a miracle or of the desired answer to prayer quite acceptable. God has used my own journey to impress deeply on me some key biblical principles. A look at a few of these will be helpful.

God Allows Pain

The promise that God always loves us is very clear in the Bible, but this same loving God allows his children to go through pain. This is a basic reality for Christians. It is the message of Scripture from Genesis through Revelation. As a child, I learned this early in my Christian faith journey. God delights in providing for the needs of his children. We are called to seek first his kingdom and righteousness and all other things will be provided (Matt. 6:25-34). I have believed that all of my life.

My life journey has taught me, as I believe no other way could have, the blessing of pain. For the first thirty-five years of my life, I worked for a holy God whom I saw as one who sat on the throne ready to pounce on my mistakes, the perfect God who expected top performance from me. Ironically, I worked hard to have God accept me while I eloquently preached that one didn't have to do anything to be accepted by God. I preached salvation by grace and practiced salvation by works, and I never saw the gross inconsistency. I was blinded to the reality that I was trying to save myself. I always felt inadequate. I felt I had never done enough and never really measured up. Deep peace and contentment were not present. If joy was a feeling, I wasn't enjoying it!

The roots for that behavior were deep and, like some wisdom teeth, were hard to remove. But by God's grace they have been removed. My own journey of pain and gradual healing played a major part in my understanding that God, in his love for me, was using pain for my good, to shape me personally and for ministry. At the time I did not see that. Instead I prayed many times for a miracle that would heal the pain and grant "the peace of God, which transcends all understanding" (Phil. 4:7). Many times I tried to bargain with God, insisting that without internal pain and with a greater sense of peace I would be more effective for him. I felt for that reason he owed me relief, if not a miracle.

It was because of the pain that I looked more intensely for God. I dug into the Word and opened myself up to others. God used those very means to teach me and remind me that he loved me unconditionally, totally unrelated to my performance. God's love for me is not determined by the correctness of my theology or by how diligently I perform my ministry. I learned to take risks, make mistakes, and fail, and when I did, accept forgiveness. The certainty of God's love empowers me to declare the promises of God, pray for healing, anoint with oil, expect God to heal, but not be shattered or feel like a failure when healing does not occur. It is really God's decision. God knows the total picture in *every* situation; I only see glimpses. So if a miracle occurs, I am deeply touched and thankful, but if not, that is OK too. God knows best and I don't. God does not have to share his plan with me, even though there are times when I really wish to know it. Ministry success is not dependent upon whether God does what I ask every time I come to him with my own or another's need.

God Suffers When We Experience Pain

There are times when sicknesses persist regardless of how many people pray—and when addictions defy victory, when temptations defeat, and when bondages cripple freedom and joy. How does a loving God deal with this?

As a father, I hated the times when one of my children was not well. Their minor pain brought a major response from me, especially when they were small and helpless. As a parent I did all I could to alleviate pain, reduce infection, heal wounds, or lift discouragement. I searched for solutions from doctors and drugstores, from hospitals or counselors. Whatever it took, I went after it with heart, soul, mind, and strength. If we, being sinful, help our children and seek healing for them, how much more does our heavenly Father, who is perfect and sinless, seek healing for his children? Nowhere in Scripture does God delight in human suffering. God grieves with us as we suffer from illnesses and tragedies. Jesus, God's Son, wept when he stood at the grave of Lazarus (John 11:35). If God says, "I take no pleasure in the death of the wicked" (Ezek. 33:11), God certainly takes no pleasure in the suffering of his children! God allows suffering and uses it. The entire book of Job illustrates this. As with Job, pain has a strange way of drawing us closer to God and making us more tender, accepting, forgiving, and loving toward others.

Many people find this area of theology confusing. Many have been taught that God has sent suffering, sickness, and pain for our good as a test to shape us into God's image. To pray for healing was always done tentatively—one does not want to interfere with God's "perfect" plan. I too was careful to cover all the theological angles and never prayed for healing without adding "not my will, but yours be done" (Luke 22:42). But that's a misuse of the words that Jesus prayed in the Garden of Gethsemane. Because of the pain that Jesus knew would accompany his death, Jesus had asked not to drink the cup of suffering. For God to answer "yes" to that prayer would have meant that the entire plan of salvation would be scuttled. So Jesus surrendered, knowing that his request was not God's will.

God doesn't always heal. Paul asked God three times to remove the "thorn in my flesh, a messenger of Satan, to torment me" (2 Cor. 12:7). Paul explained that God's refusal to remove the thorn was intended "to keep me from becoming conceited." He added God's promise: "My grace is sufficient for you, for my power is made perfect in weakness" (v. 9). It's a passage often used to prove that healing is *not* the will of God. These rather isolated texts are offset by the gospels, which use about one verse in every seven to portray God's will to heal. In Acts, it is one in fourteen. One small passage dealing with an unremovable "thorn in the flesh" designed to foster humility and reliance on God's grace cannot undo all other New Testament teaching.

The entire ministry of Christ was a demonstration of God's love. When reading the gospels we note that, when people came to Christ for healing, they were healed. Jesus never turned anyone away, nor was any illness too tough for him to heal. At times, Jesus left behind some who had come for healing simply because he needed to move on to other communities (see, for example, Mark 1:35-39). The good news of the kingdom had to be shared with others for whom Jesus had also come. Though Jesus assaults sin, suffering, and death, they remain a part of the human condition called "life." That sober reality needs to be acknowledged by all, including Christians. Perfect healing and the fullness of redemption will come. In the meantime we face the inevitable and rely on God's Spirit to comfort us in our sufferings.

Suffering Is Inevitable

Immense suffering and pain surround us. No smile can cover the pain; no parties, jokes, or optimism can remove the wounds and disappointments of life. Sooner or later, each of us is touched directly. The longer we live, the more certain the pain. Death stalks and attacks us at shockingly unexpected times. Accidents happen, sicknesses come to us and our loved ones. For those who live to a ripe old age, suffering deepens as they watch friends die. As a pastor it has struck me deeply when older people tell me that with a measure of dread they turn to the obituary page of their local newspaper wondering which one of their friends or acquaintances they are going to read about next. The last enemy, death, waits like a vulture to have us.

When my doctor told me I had inoperable cancer, I was numb and shocked. "It can't be me," I thought in disbelief. "I have work to do—I'm a fifth-grade teacher, a Children and Worship leader. . . . These children need me, and I need them." As I tried to comprehend what my doctor said, she reached for my hands and led in prayer.

Within an hour after hearing the news, friends from church and school came to my home. They came to offer whatever they could—to share in the sadness and to pray and lift me up before God. What an awesome blessing to be in God's family!

The next week I was referred to an oncologist, and plans were made for chemotherapy. The first three treatments went remarkably well. I didn't get sick, I wasn't tired, I carried on with my teaching, and I was beginning to think chemo wasn't so bad. Then, within twenty-four hours after my fourth treatment, I became deathly sick. I spent five days in the hospital and then went home with hospice care. The doctor wasn't sure what the problem was until a short time later when I lost all the skin on my hands, fingers, and soles of my feet. Instead of metabolizing the chemo, my body was storing the chemo in the cells and filling my fragile body with toxic poisons. Chemotherapy was out!

For a brief moment I thought, "Now what? Surgery isn't an option because of the advanced cancer, chemo doesn't work. What then?" Just like that, God said: "Do not fear, for I am with you; do not be dismayed, for I am your God. I will strengthen you and help you; I will uphold you with my righteous right hand" (Isa. 41:10).

Society tries to avoid and escape pain. Many in our culture live in denial until death breaks into their circles. Even then, everything is done to make death as nice as possible. We have beautiful chapels, fancy coffins, copious flowers, and we "rest our beloved in a garden of peace." All the niceties do not remove the pain caused by the brutal separation of death. It lasts for years; in fact, some never recover from the loss of a spouse or a child. Christians tend to gloss over this as we too tend to live with a measure of denial. It seems as if we believe that pain and the Christian life are inconsistencies, so we discourage each other from honest expressions of pain, grief, or sadness. Somehow, we think that does not fit the Christian life. Honesty in these areas is viewed as a poor witness, or worse, a lack of faith and trust in God. This often results in huge amounts of lonely, quiet suffering, much of which would be decreased if only it were shared. The Bible clearly teaches that life for God's children can be very painful. In many instances the source of the pain can be identified; in others it cannot. Well-meaning Christians add to the pain with their quick and ready explanations.

I thank God for the ceaseless prayers on my behalf. I envision all these prayers ascending to the throne of God—what an awesome picture. When I was too sick to pray, my family and friends prayed. They knew how close to death I was, and I can only say that God heard their prayers and performed a miracle. My heart feels such joy and thankfulness.

My life is in God's hands. Each day I pray, hope, and wait in expectation of what God is going to do. My heart's desire is to be healed of cancer so that I can teach again. I see all the children in kindergarten, first, second, third, and fourth grades, and I want to be their fifth grade teacher so I can point them to Jesus. God says, "Be still, and know that I am God" (Ps. 46:10).

I am in God's waiting room. Waiting allows me plenty of time to listen, to pray, and to celebrate God's faithfulness. I've read the reports of the malignancy, and I sense the seriousness of it all. Some days I have to battle the "what ifs." Then I call on the "reserves" to help me—my prayer partners are part of God's army. I need them to pray that God will keep me patient, encouraged and hopeful in this battle against cancer. God has the strategy laid out. God will trample down the enemy and bring me to victory. All praise to God!

—Dorothy DeBoer. Used with permission.

"Dot" DeBoer taught at Bradenton Christian School in Bradenton, Florida, for twenty-nine years. She served for many years as a church education consultant and was a member of the board for CRC Publications. She was also a trainer for Children and Worship. Dot went to be with her heavenly Father on Father's Day, 1999.

While some Christians live with denial, others flippantly ascribe all this hell on earth to the devil. They credit Satan with the creation of all this havoc. If that is so, where is God? Sitting by helplessly as we cry, grieve, and suffer? What does that do to our image of a perfect God?

Satan is involved with the suffering experienced by all. For some Christians this is clearly a black-and-white issue: Satan is evil, suffering is bad, it comes from the evil one; God is good, miracles are good, they come from God. They believe that the right response to pain is to pray for healing and restoration as quickly as possible. God will eagerly perform miracles to rebuke Satan's afflictions because all sickness is evil and contrary to God's will. These Christians say we need to pray and believe and the affliction will be gone; if not, weak or absent faith hindered the healing. Many other Christians have been deeply hurt by this unrealistic condensing of serious issues that defy such simple explanations. It's also laid huge guilt trips on serious, God-serving brothers and sisters.

We acknowledge that God allows sin, sickness, suffering, and death to afflict us. They molest and plague us our entire lives. And the fall into sin made death inevitable (Gen. 3). Our clocks were started at that moment, and ever since then every human being has lived with the tension of constantly racing the clock. We wind down as our allotment of days winds down. We are born to die; life is a fatal disease—and honestly admitting that allows us to be most realistic with ourselves, most helpful to others, and most direct with God in our prayer life.

The inevitable leaves a gloomy picture. If that is all there is to life, no wonder our hospitals are filled with people who have given up and would bail out if they knew how. Should we be surprised when we meet malaise or despair? For a world in despair, God provides a message of hope.

The Best Is Yet to Be!

Redemption has come. Centuries of waiting and watching were fulfilled with the birth of Christ. The ugly reality of sin and death is being removed from us as we live by faith in the Son of God. God forgives and renews. God heals and restores what has been lost. But the last enemy waits and seems to gain another victory every time someone dies.

Not so! It appears that way—but this time appearances are deceiving! We live with a tension: we are forgiven and redeemed, yet we suffer and die. Hope, faith, courage, and confidence floods our lives when we reflect on our status in Christ. But quickly and unexpectedly that confident courage is shattered when we hit another wall of disappointment, a week-long migraine, or a relationship breakdown that should never have happened. Redemption is *here,* but it is also very much *not yet.* At death or at the time of the return of Christ, consummation of perfect salvation occurs. What we now understand so poorly becomes the grand surprise.

In the meantime, the new community of Christ—the church—is assigned the task to preach the good news and to portray healing and reconciliation. The church demonstrates the better way, but also that the best is yet to be. Believers show what it is to know and enjoy a Lord who *is* redeemer now. Christ is also the risen Lord who does miracles and through them portrays God's love. He can be called upon for help. Jesus waits to heal and longs to bless. His goodness is unlimited, and he offers more than we are often ready to receive.

There's much room for growth in these areas. Many members and leaders in our congregations are eager to move forward in these areas. In recent years, we have seen a remarkable growth in the emphasis upon prayer. Many churches now have regular services of prayer and various prayer meetings. Participants are developing a deep awareness that God hears and answers the pleas of his people. In that light, how can the church develop further the ministry of healing?

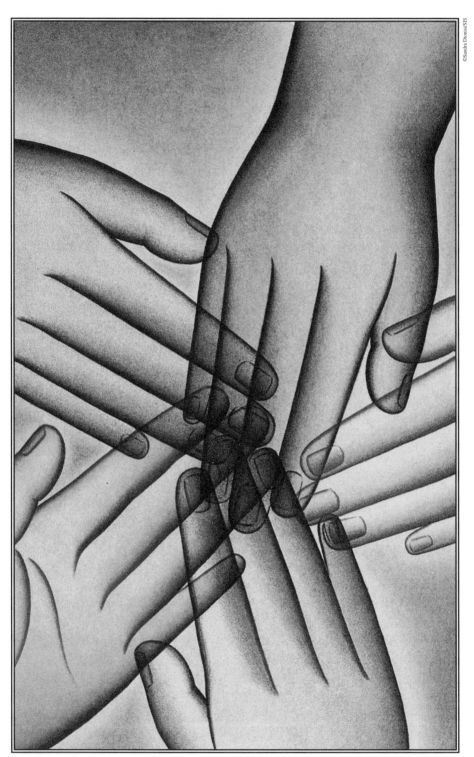

Five Hands

—Sandra Dionisi, 20th C.

CHAPTER 9

HEALING MINISTRIES AND THE LEADERSHIP

Because many people in traditional, mainline churches have had limited exposure to miracles and experience with prayer for healing, wisdom calls for patience, love, and gentle guidance. This must come from pastors and other leaders in the church.

Some pastors and leaders will be cautious—in an area as controversial as this, super cautious! Some leaders will urge the pastor to leave the subject alone even when miracles are affecting members. Pain and fear causes them to ask, "Why raise a controversial issue?" That may well be wise advice if the church has been through a period of tension, if there is a lack of trust in the leadership, or if unity within the congregation is fragile. For some leaders this reaction means a temporary hold; for others, it confirms their permanent stance, rigidly held and promoted. But if the subject of miracles and healings has invaded the hearts and lives of the membership, leaders may well need to be proactive. Relevant biblical preaching and teaching play a significant role.

Preaching and Teaching

Ideally, it's good planning to do a sermon series on miracles when no controversy exists. But emergencies and cries for help rarely follow well-planned liturgical schedules. Though wisdom may dictate that you postpone handling the issue publicly, particularly in a time of conflict, that is not always possible. It is often exactly at such times that urgent requests for prayer for healing are received. Interest escalates exponentially when someone in the congregation who is seriously ill asks for prayer and experiences a dramatic healing. This creates "hot potato" discussions and debates; then a related message can be carefully heard, digested, and discussed. Tape recordings of such messages, in fact, travel far beyond the local congregation. The pastor needs to be open to the fact that he or she will not have the last word on the subject; the pulpit ministry should enhance discussion and not stifle it.

Specific situations do arise in the life of the church when teaching is needed in a particular area. Those sometimes are areas God's people prefer to avoid. A subtle resistance is common, prompting leaders to avoid dealing with a problem, sin, or habit rampant in the congregation, especially if it is volatile. Fear, blindness, or even hardness in the leader's heart may also cause avoidance of certain areas. The fear or cost of change has the uncanny ability to shut out truths that confront long-standing sinful practices. Teaching or preaching on

A member of my church, whom I'll call Dick, had been influenced by the charismatic movement. Dick suffered from ongoing abdominal pains. The pain was constantly severe; at times it was excruciating.

One Saturday afternoon, Dick gave me a letter addressed to my church elders. The day before he had received the results of a long series of medical tests indicating no specific reason for the pain. Specialists had agreed that exploratory surgery was warranted and had scheduled it for the following Wednesday morning. Dick's letter asked us to implement James 5 and to please do so before Wednesday. Time for calm, exegetical studies and theological reflection was out. The question was quite simple: "Will you or will you not?" For Dick it was more than a theological question; it was an issue of faith and hope. We realized that.

As elders we read his letter and wondered how to respond. What about the passage? Does it still apply? Do we read it literally? What about the oil, and what kind of oil? One elder asked, "What could we possibly do wrong if we simply did what the passage said?" This wisdom prevailed. We agreed to meet Dick at church on Sunday afternoon, and elders "comfortable with doing this" were invited to join. All came—some with great faith and expectations, some out of curiosity, others with skepticism.

We gathered around Dick and read the Scripture passage as well as some other passages dealing with the healings of Jesus. We shared with each other our fears and our desire for greater faith. We confessed our feelings of foolishness as we anointed with oil, our inability to really understand how God could use this ritual and prayer for healing. We were honest, open, and vulnerable. After about twenty minutes of sharing and confession, we anointed Dick's forehead with oil, laid hands on him, and prayed. About half of the elders verbalized their thoughts and doubts in the prayer. We ended, went home, and left it at that.

Within a day, Dick's pain decreased, and it was completely gone by Wednesday, the day for which surgery was scheduled. The doctors postponed the surgery and later canceled it. We were amazed! And the pain never returned.

—Henry Wildeboer

healing often raises these and other complicated issues. It can arouse unresolved conflicts or stir up hidden bitterness associated with a lack of forgiveness. Healing is a vast subject and covers many dimensions in the life of a church family.

Preaching about and praying for specific miracles may bring surprising results. One may well ask, "Should we take the risk? Why not avoid the controversial?" I confess I have done that, but often with regret. If we are committed to teaching the whole counsel of God, can we in good conscience avoid this topic? Personally I've noted that every time I preached on the subject of healing and provided an opportunity for prayer, members responded and some were healed. When I taught the church about the importance of the prayer of faith and the anointing with oil described in James 5:13-16, some requested that ministry and were healed. Some were not, and at times we were left with puzzling questions. Would it not have been better to leave the issue alone? Does it not raise false hopes? John Wimber of Vineyard fame, in a class at Fuller Seminary, stated that when he prayed for healing the best result was God healing the person, often to his surprise. Even when healing did not occur, the person felt loved and sensed others struggling with him.

There are times when all the biblical requirements are scrupulously met and healing should have happened but didn't. We do not know why. At such times, with deep reluctance, the matter is surrendered to the sovereignty of God. We painfully acknowledge that we are puzzled, that our inadequate human understanding is unable to grasp the reasoning of an almighty God. Though we confess with our minds that God does all things well, at such times we simply do not experience that reality!

Preaching and teaching in this area is vital to a Bible-believing church. A number of series are possible. Old Testament miracles abound. A series on miracles in the lives of Elijah (1 Kings 17-19) and Elisha (2 Kings 2-8) will include healings and other miracles. Some can be included from the life of Christ and from the book of Acts. Miracles are part of the good news of salvation, the new life, and the coming of God's kingdom in a world that is self-centered and self-serving. Regular teaching in these areas results in other changes.

Teaching from James Today?

With greater regularity, church members ask for the application of the teaching of James 5 in cases of illnesses and injuries. What are pastors and church leaders to do with the teaching as outlined in this "Prayer of Faith" passage:

> Is any one of you in trouble? He should pray. Is anyone happy? Let him sing songs of praise. Is any one of you sick? He should call the elders of the church to pray over him and anoint him with oil in the name of the Lord. And the prayer offered in faith will make the sick person well; the Lord will raise him up. If he has sinned, he will be forgiven. Therefore confess your sins to each other and pray for each other so that you may be healed. The prayer of a righteous man is powerful and effective.
>
> —James 5:13-16

This is a troublesome issue for many people. Is it to be taken literally? Should it be practiced today? Or, is it a culturally conditioned text that, because of medical advances, is now outdated? Many today think that the oil served a medicinal purpose in the times of James, and that it has been replaced by better health care and federally approved prescription drugs. People adopt this position without really questioning it. Occasionally, while reading through the book of James, I came across the verse but did not slow down enough to ask "What about today?" A very practical experience (see Dick's story on p. 74) forced me to take a closer

My illness started in 1967 when I was thirty-four years old. I was enjoying my work at General Motors, supporting my wife and three children, the oldest of whom was nine years old. Numbness in my leg and blinding in one eye led me to my doctor. He suspected a possible blockage in my spine, but wisely had me hospitalized for tests. There they discovered that I was afflicted with the debilitating disease multiple sclerosis, commonly called MS.

I was unable to work for about twelve months. From 1968 to 1976 the MS continued its course of depleting my life and energy. I experienced periods of paralysis of my limbs and loss of coordination. I would work for a few months, suffer another attack, lose more work time, return until the next bout. Each attack meant more loss of strength and stamina. In 1976, I came to the dreaded moment when I and others realized that my deteriorating condition precipitated an early, unavoidable retirement. At the youthful age of 43, I was retired and put on a disability pension.

Though I was no longer working, my disease continued to drain me. There were periods of decline followed with times of slight improvements. All in all, however, I was regressing. I realized it would only be a matter of time. The longest distance I could walk was 200 feet, and then only with the support of a cane. In 1981, I suffered another severe attack which left me very weak and tired.

In the fall of 1984, after much thought and prayer, I asked the elders of my church to anoint me with oil, lay hands on me, and pray for my healing as James 5 instructs. They responded positively and did so at the conclusion of a Sunday morning worship service. The entire congregation was made aware of the request and most of them stayed for a time of prayer while the elders fulfilled my request and prayed over me. It was an upbuilding experience for all. I felt very much affirmed and loved. I did not feel anything dramatic nor did anything change at the moment; however, since then I have never had another attack.

look at the passage and led to requests to teach and preach that passage of Scripture. I needed to work with the passage. It was good for me to do so.

A Closer Look at the "Prayer of Faith"

James begins his letter by dealing with trials (1:2), and then, approaching the end, he picks up the theme of suffering or afflictions (5:13). Some of that suffering is experienced in sickness. If you are sick, James says, call for the elders of the church. This was simply a continuation of a common practice of the

Nearly two years later, I was still using a wheelchair regularly, but I was improving ever so gradually. Over an extended period of time my strength and stamina returned. Coordination began to improve. I began to swim, take longer walks, and began cycling with great regularity, even in the winter when at all possible. In fact, I had two cycling accidents in two years. The first resulted in a broken arm, the second left me with a shattered leg. My recovery in both instances was remarkable.

I continue to improve. I now swim 30 minutes, five times per week. I walk 1.3 miles and cycle about 5 miles per day. I believe God has healed me and so gradually that it was hardly noticeable at times. Only when I look back over a longer period of time do I most clearly see the improvements. My family, my church, and I are deeply thankful for what God continues to do in my life.

In 1996, I gave my testimony regarding God's healing to the entire congregation. Five days later I became seriously ill. The doctor was unable to come up with a diagnosis but prepared me to face the fact that it might be an MS attack. I had planned to visit family in the Netherlands but was advised to cancel the trip. It was discouraging for my wife and me. We were fearful—had the MS returned? And precisely five days after my testimony? The following Sunday, I went forward to the front of the church after the worship service where a prayer ministry team prayed . . . that it would not be MS. The following week I was referred to a specialist, who also could not provide a [diagnosis]. A few days later I learned that I did not have MS but a case of shingles, which healed rather quickly. Today, 1999, I continue to improve. I am deeply grateful to God. My wife and I praise God for his goodness, shown to us in such abundant measures.

—Adri Oudyk. Used by permission.

Adri Oudyk and his wife, Leny, live in Oshawa, Ontario, Canada, where they are long-time members of Zion Christian Reformed Church.

early church. The rabbis of the Jewish community of the Old Testament and members and leaders of the church of the New Testament visited the sick.

Visiting the sick, often with a helpful gift, probably goes back to prehistoric times. It was common among the Jews (for example, see Matt. 25:43). In Jerusalem, societies of pious men attended weddings and engagement parties and visited the bereaved, even of the Gentiles. The elders' visit to the sick was already a Jewish custom, as James Adamson explains in his commentary *The Epistle of James: The New International Commentary on the New Testament* (p. 197):

> In this case, James says, the sick person should call for the elders, who are to come, pray over him, and anoint him with oil in the name of the Lord. To "pray over them" was common at that time, and is so again now, especially with the growth of the charismata. The anointing with oil is a symbol, much like the water of baptism; in itself it does not heal any more than the water of baptism washes away sins. Whatever happens occurs not so much because of the "anointing with oil" but because it is an action done *in the name of the Lord.* That's why it has significance.

Elders and pastors from other churches frequently ask whether the oil is necessary. When I inquire why they ask, they respond by saying that they feel rather "silly" putting oil on the forehead of a person. "Can't God heal without the oil?" Of course God can! But James states to anoint with oil. There is nothing dangerous or damaging about it, so why not do it? Anointing with oil is a humbling act. That's why it so hard, and yet so good, to do it. It is also symbolic in that in a sacramental way it portrays the presence of the Spirit.

In dealing with the pride matter, I frequently refer to Naaman (2 Kings 5), who came to Elisha to be healed from the horrible disease of leprosy. When Elisha sent out his servant, who told Naaman to go and wash himself seven times in the river Jordan, Naaman became furious. The Jordan was dirty compared to the Abana and Pharpar rivers in Damascus, and the command to wash seven times could be better fulfilled at home! Naaman's pride was wounded, and he was ready to return home until a servant confronted him and asked, "What have you got to lose?" The big question for Naaman (and frequently for Christians today) is this: "Are we willing to look foolish in the presence of others for God's sake?" Amazing exegetical calisthenics are performed in order *not* to anoint with oil. As with Naaman, there is nothing to lose and much to gain spiritually, even when God doesn't heal! Why not simply do it?

After giving specific directions about prayer and the anointing, James matter-of-factly adds, "And the prayer offered in faith will make the sick person well; the Lord will raise him up. If he has sinned, he will be forgiven" (James

5:15). The entire emphasis is on the power of God who heals illness and forgives sins. Sin and sickness travel together, and the Lord is redeemer and healer for both of them. The prayer accompanied by faith accomplishes amazing things. In fact, verses 17 and 18 describe how Elijah's prayer stopped and started the rains. Faith is always an asset for healing, even though there are various miracles in which it is not mentioned, as we noted in chapter 2.

"Therefore confess your sins to each other and pray for each other so that you may be healed," James continues in verse 16. Amazingly, this verse starts with the Greek word *oun,* translated *therefore.* It is directly connected with what has gone before and is addressed to the elders who were called by the sick person. Note the only thing that the sick person does is call for the elders. That's all you can expect someone who is sick to do. Everything else in the passage is directed to the community. They are to confess their sins to each other. Why? Let's look at two reasons.

- First, sin causes brokenness and disruption.

  Psalm 66:18 teaches that sin "cherished" in our hearts but unconfessed hinders the Lord from hearing our prayers. Sin and broken relationships strain the community. God calls elders to be one in heart, commitment, and ministry. Where people live together in unity, "there the LORD bestows his blessing" (Ps. 133:3). Standing around the sickbed of a member, anointing with oil, and then preparing to pray for healing is a unifying experience, especially when those called to do that first confess their sins to each other. Unresolved conflicts, failure to repent, and a lack of forgiveness are mountainous obstacles that are sometimes more easily resolved in a setting in which unity is a must. Much depends upon it. It's phony to pray together when relationships are tattered. So before praying together for healing of the sick, be one in your relationships. That in itself is a major healing.

- Second, the elders are to pray *in faith.*

  Unbelief is a hindrance to healing. In fact, a lack of faith, often expressed by fears and doubts, displeases the Lord. His words—"you of little faith" (Matt. 8:26)—ring in our hearts. For elders to confess the weakness of their faith and the presence of fear and doubt is humbling and unifying, and the very confession helps to remove those faults. The prayer is meant as much to increase the elders' trust and faith in God as it is to heal the person who called them to come. The prayer of confession before each other and God will first heal those who pray, as verse 16 states. It deepens their faith and intensifies the boldness with which they come to God to ask for healing for the one who is sick. In those instances, we might well be surprised had healing *not* occurred.

Guaranteed Results?

Is a miracle guaranteed when we follow the steps precisely outlined in James 5? If the answer could be "yes" to that we'd have a neat formula! But God will not be put into a box. God retains the freedom to say yes or no.

We have seen a number of instances in which amazing healings have occurred. Almost humorously, this is often the case the first time a group of elders responds to the request and acts upon it. But there are also puzzling instances when all the conditions were fully met, but no relief or healing resulted. I wish I knew why. I don't. It has troubled me deeply and has led to introspection. I have wondered about our faith in such instances and have questioned whether the text still applies. Does the passage need to be revisited exegetically? Should we respond differently to requests? But what about times when God did reverse debilitating illnesses? As in other areas, Christians will continue to live with unanswered questions.

As Christians we confess that all of the Scriptures need to be taught. That includes James 5:13-16. When we get specific requests to implement the teaching of the passage, we do what the Bible says as fully and accurately as possible. We leave the results with God without feeling that we are accountable to have to explain what God does. When God heals, let there be joy. When God doesn't heal, let there be love and compassion to support the person even when walking through the valley of the shadow of death. The sovereign Lord does all things well. Though God is always faithful, God is not always predictable.

We cannot lose when we combine the wisdom and sovereignty of God with this simple confession: "I am not my own, but belong—body and soul, in life and death—to my faithful Savior Jesus Christ" (*The Heidelberg Catechism,* Lord's Day 1). Or as the apostle Paul says, "in all these things we are more than conquerors through him who loved us" (Rom. 8:37). Though it is easy to confess when all is well, it is equally true when things are not well. To accept the goodness of God when God does not heal is also a matter of faith. Constant confidence in God, regardless of circumstances, provides stability, confidence, and courage to face the future. Leaders need to model and teach that.

Even though pastors and leaders in churches show an openness to God's miraculous work today, this area of ministry is not limited to them. Sickness and other trials come to *all* members. Continuing in prayer and growing in faith is God's challenge to *every* Christian. The ministry of God and the gifts of God are shared with all, providing many opportunities for the involvement of those who may never take part in leadership responsibilities. They look for help, encouragement, and direction from their leaders. What can be done? How can they better be released for the ministries to which God is calling them? That warrants the final chapter.

People Joining Hands, detail

—Tim Grajek, 20th C.

CHAPTER 10

HEALING MINISTRIES
AND THE CONGREGATION

If we accept that miracles continue to happen and if we acknowledge God's amazing interventions in certain cases of illness, we need to ask, "How can church members be directly involved in this ministry?" If the church is to proclaim the Word of God that all readily profess, is the church also called to do the works of God? Reformed Christians have always answered that question with a resounding "yes." But doing the works of God has usually meant extending God's kingdom in the areas of education, politics, justice, evangelism, and so on. It has not typically included the miraculous healing of the sick.

Because there is considerable confusion and fear about miraculous healing, many people prefer to avoid the issue and would like the church to follow the same practice. Or, if the church is to be involved, they want it to be a ministry for the leaders and the "super-spiritual." Though that approach is not uncommon, it is unrealistic and does not do justice to the Scriptures nor to the times in which we are living. Christians in all churches sooner or later will face these matters, and either they will be helped by their own churches or they will go elsewhere for input. Our contacts with others do not allow us the luxury to "stick our heads in the sand" and pretend that nothing is happening. Church members will not be ignorant about this. They want to know, they want to be involved—and they can be.

Faithful Teaching about Healing

Faithful biblical teaching about healing is crucial because of the environment in which we live. Shysters, hucksters, and show-off healers have made significant inroads into our Christian communities. Some Christians tell awesome stories; others tell awful stories about healing miracles. Many members repeat fake miracle stories with great hilarity. The possibility of real miracles brings out counterfeits.

Confusion about God's involvement and responsibility for illness, our own fears, and the reluctance or unwillingness of our church leaders to deal with the issue of healing has allowed huge voids to grow in the hearts of church members. In times when things are well, they are open and searching for new experiences; in times of pain, the hunger for relief leaves members vulnerable to being sucked into manipulative schemes. An openness to genuine miracles, combined with careful biblical theology and a discerning spirit to separate the phony healer from the real, provides good protection against deception. The church can also be a safe place for struggles, questions, and experimentation in this area of illness, prayer, and faith that asks and expects God to hear and heal. Rather than respond reluctantly and fearfully to those who ask for help, as Christian leaders we might well lead the way! How can that be done?

The influence of charismatics and ecumenical contacts with other Christians have resulted in Reformed Christians reevaluating the basics of what they believe. They know that healing services are now more common in traditional, conservative, mainline churches. They know that elders *and* members are laying hands on the sick—some with the anointing of oil—and asking God for healing. And God is blessing their actions. Many evangelical and Reformed churches now have inspiring testimonies about how God has answered prayers and has miraculously intervened.

For prayer for healing to have a unifying impact, the church might well share a common consensus on a few basic issues. The following five foundational principles have been helpful.

- The Bible portrays God's great compassion for human brokenness.

  God demonstrates the power of his love in a great variety of ways, including through miracles (see chapter 4). As we pointed out in chapter 5, Jesus' healings also showed deep compassion for the suffering.

- Adequate faith is not a prerequisite to healing in all instances.

  We noted in chapter 2 that Jesus' healings were not limited to those who had faith. It's dangerous to generalize. Devastating stories circulate in the Christian community of guilt trips laid on sick people who were told that they would have been healed if they had only had more faith.

- Miracles and healings occurred before, during, and after the coming of Christ.

  The disciples and the apostolic church continued to experience miracles after Christ's ascension (see chapters 6 and 7). No Scripture passage states that miracles are limited to any specific era. Some use the familiar passage "Prophecies . . . will cease; . . . tongues . . . will be stilled; . . . knowledge . . . will pass away" (1 Cor. 13:8) to support their view that gifts and miracles have ceased. The text, however, refers to Christ's return "when perfection comes" (v. 10) and we will see the full picture rather than a shaded reflection. We will then know all things as we ourselves will also be fully open and known (v. 12). This passage is *not* a reference to the passing away of gifts and miracles after the New Testament era. The church in Corinth could not possibly have understood these verses as referring to the completion of the New Testament Canon.

- Initiating a ministry of healing need not wait until we can explain why healings occur in some instances and not in others.

  As we acknowledged in chapter 8, God allows sin, sickness, suffering, and death. Perfect healing and the fullness of redemption are the best that is yet to be!

- Involvement in a ministry of healing may lead to criticism, labeling, and even scorn.

  This is particularly true for leaders and members of a congregation that is viewed as classy or sophisticated or is known for well-articulated theological positions, carefully planned worship services, and socially relevant ministries.

Developing a Healing Ministry

Can a traditional evangelical or Reformed congregation become more actively involved in a healing ministry? Peter Wagner's book entitled *How to Have a Healing Ministry Without Making Your Church Sick!* says that there are steps that can be taken to develop an effective, accepted ministry. Ministries can be implemented with patience, gentleness, and minimal resistance if the church has the luxury of gradually moving into this area. But preaching and teaching are often colored by issues that are already stirring a church's members. Many pastors find themselves addressing the issue of healing after it has entered the church through others in the community. Or it may suddenly arise when a major illness creates a crisis in the church. In either of these cases, interest is high and positions are often taken before anyone asks what the scriptural perspective might be.

Rather than reacting defensively, both leaders and members can be intentional about dealing with illness and developing a ministry of healing. I firmly believe that healing ministries need to be initiated in more congregations. Healings, conversions, and other miracles occur more frequently in settings in which there is intense prayer. God still answers the prayers of the righteous (James 5:16). The following five suggestions develop the theme of prayer and will, we may hope, deepen the fellowship among members. These suggestions are very much based upon my own experience.

- Invite prayer requests.

  True preaching and teaching produces hearing that leads to doing. If members are going to make changes, leaders need to lead the way, and that includes in the area of worship. I felt awkward the first time, when, at the end of a worship service, I stated, "If any of you have needs or illnesses and you'd like prayer for healing, please come forward." I really didn't expect anyone to move. But in fact, that time and every time since, when people were given an opportunity to respond, they did! Members were far more eager to seek help than I as a leader was prepared to give it. Requests for specific prayer for healing increased as our expectations changed. We've been reminded again and again that we have not because we ask not, and we ask not because we expect not! It *really* is a matter of faith!

Encouraging members to make prayer requests during the worship services makes prayer more practical and more accessible to the person in the pew. As a prayer ministry develops and becomes a more natural part of the church's life, the desire and requests for prayer will also increase. Members will begin to pray for each other. They will more frequently ask others to pray for them and become bolder about such requests even in public settings.

In my congregations, the more we prayed, the better the results—some joyous surprises. We also began to pray before we had answers to all our questions. The calls for help led to stepping out in faith and obedience. Sometimes we just laid the requests before God without doing a lot of analyzing. The prayers resulted in amazing responses. Many times we neither understood nor could explain what had happened—we just knew that God's Spirit was at work among us. We became more flexible, all part of doing theology "on the run."

- Develop prayer groups.

Series of sermons on the subject of prayer *in* church services often resulted in members forming prayer groups *outside* the church. Some started spontaneously in homes; others met at the church or at restaurants. Many members seem to have a great desire for a deeper life with God and for a fellowship that is intentional about praying together.

In many churches only a bit of encouragement is needed for groups to form prayer circles. Christians involved in Bible studies, especially women's groups, share needs and are often quite open to praying together. Many have formed prayer chains that meet specific needs as they occur. The person in need or a family member calls a publicized phone number to ask for prayer; the person receiving the request calls the next person, and so on all the way around the chain until the last member calls the first person again. Each person is committed to pray for the need and to retain confidentiality.

In many small groups and other Bible studies, participants are constantly confronted with the importance of prayer. The Spirit, working through the Word, convicts many about this often neglected aspect of spiritual vitality. As they begin to pray and meet others with similar convictions, members' hearts are stirred and their spirituality is enriched. This increases the longing to drink more deeply. For many, prayer, spiritual vitality, and strong relationships are directly intertwined. Occasionally confidences will be broken, but where integrity and openness are present, these instances can be handled readily. Members committed to prayer are usually open to correction or suggestions for improvement without becoming defensive. Leaders can surely support this enthusiastically.

- Organize prayer support teams.

Increased interest in prayer provides opportunities to develop prayer support teams, sometimes referred to as intercessors. Every church seems to have a number of people who desire to pray and intercede for others. It is an immense blessing for a leader to be supported in prayer by a small group of people who intercede on a daily basis. At times leaders can share specific congregational needs with the team; at other times more general situations. Some know me so well that they pray intensely for me Saturday night through Sunday morning, an invariably "low" time for me spiritually just before I preach or lead worship. Knowing that one has constant prayer support provides strength and courage. When one is facing a major issue or a crucial decision, a reassuring phone call from an active, strong prayer group is essential.

Members also do that for each other. In fact, every leader and teacher in our present congregation has a team of intercessors who pray for that person and his or her ministry. When needs arise, God is petitioned; when problems are resolved, God is praised. The overall result is that more people experience the importance of prayer and see answers to prayer. That boosts the level of faith and creates greater boldness that asks and expects more from God.

In that kind of prayer setting it is relatively easy to implement prayer teams that minister to members and visitors after worship services. It has become standard practice in some congregations to have two to five teams of two people move to the front of the auditorium at the end of the service to pray with anyone who so desires. Visitors are amazed and sense a deep love when they hear this announcement:

> If you have a need or if you would like someone to pray with you, feel free to come to the front of the church or go to our prayer room. We have people who are prepared to pray with you. Whether a visitor or member, feel free to come. You'll only be asked one question: "What would you like God to do for you?"

Preparing teams for intercessory ministry has not been difficult. Volunteers are easy to find. Some are husband-and-wife teams, a beautiful ministry for a couple. Others work together as a team just for the ministry of prayer.

We were a hodgepodge group of volunteers who found ourselves serving on a committee dealing with a huge and complex issue for our church. We varied widely in gifts and temperament. After our leader unexpectedly quit, it was unclear what would happen. Whose vision would prevail?

Together we decided to pray.... Often we spent an hour of our meeting time in prayer. Chiefly as a result of the extended prayer times, our group found a unity we never expected. We discovered that we wanted God's plan above our own preferences.... We felt we were truly part of God's blessing for our church.

And our church has been in need of blessing. Oakdale Park Christian Reformed Church is a diverse, inner-city congregation of about four hundred members that is evolving from a traditional ethnic enclave into a neighborhood church. Through—and because of—our struggles, prayer is beginning to form the foundation of all we do.

We are beginning to get an inkling of the power that lies in prayer. It has taken us some time to learn that prayer is not one activity among many in which we are to engage. Rather, it is the central action through which all other ministries—worship included—receive power and direction....

Because of our growth in prayer outside the sanctuary, we have learned also to pray together with increasing frequency and growing participation in our worship. We are getting used to praying out loud and with each other in smaller groups. Prayer has become a much more natural part of our being together. This spills over into our congregational worship as well....

We have done much over the past six to eight years to make prayer a central part of our congregational life, worship, and ministry. But we have just begun to scratch the surface of this powerful gift that God has given us.

If you are hoping to make prayer a larger part of your church's future ministry too, you will need a few people with a vision for prayer. That was all we started with. God does the rest.

—Excerpts from "Together We Decided to Pray" by Edith Bajema, *Reformed Worship*, June 1999, pp. 6-7. Used by permission.

Edith Bajema is active in the prayer and worship ministries of Oakdale Park Christian Reformed Church, Grand Rapids, Michigan. She is a freelance writer and editor and the mother of three teenage children.

Establishing some basic guidelines (for example, males minister to males, females to females) and reaffirming fundamental listening and questioning skills will help team members feel comfortable. The most important requirement is for the teams to know how to talk to God. All they need to do is to take what they hear, tell it to the Father, and ask for God's help, strength, or healing. Emphasize that God does the work; teams simply share the needs in short, simple prayers. Intercessory prayer time is *not* a counseling session.

- Share answers to prayer.

The theological truth that God answers prayer is not always a living reality in people's hearts. Every Christian has instances of answered prayer in their lives that few others know about. Sharing the stories of God's work in our lives encourages others. When we hear that God has healed another person, we become bolder in asking God for help in our lives. Nothing encourages a congregation to become a praying church more than stories in which God met crucial needs. If members are prayed for by prayer teams or by intercessors, it is inspiring to hear about answers. Provide regular opportunities for members to share the results of prayer for those willing to do so.

On some occasions, God's family needs to be encouraged to take risks and to step out in faith. Though scary, and perhaps too subjective for some, God's Spirit convicts us at times to ask boldly and confidently. The gift of faith that provides confidence or boldness may be present with one or two but not all. Personally, I have been present when we prayed for healing, and I knew when we finished praying that it was done! I have prayed for young couples to be blessed with a child, and in some instances knew when we finished praying that it would happen. But there are also memories of instances when we prayed equally fervently and God said no. Our inability to explain the difference makes us hesitate to take risks.

We need to share God's answers to our prayer. God's healing blessings raise our level of faith and expectations. But this also becomes an area that tests integrity. Leaders and pastors eager to develop strong prayer ministries are tempted to share only desirable answers. What happens when the desired answer does not come? What is shared at such times? The silence can be embarrassing. Prayers were "asked in faith," but did God not come through? If others hear about this, will they be shattered in their faith and perhaps conclude that the whole prayer thing is a hoax? It is honest and upbuilding to also share when the answer sought was not the answer received and to publicly acknowledge that we do not understand, that we have no explanation except to say that God is God, and that our humanity does not call for an explanation from our sovereign God.

Amazingly, lives are not shattered when the lack of the desired results are shared humbly and honestly. When a person dies even after a church anoints him with oil and prays fervently with much faith and courage, all wonder what happened, whether they express it or not. Credibility and integrity develop when leaders open up, express honestly their own disappointment, and allow others to do the same. Our congregation was deeply stirred when we admitted our pain and struggle over a funeral service that, humanly speaking, should not have been. The admission resulted in greater admiration for the awesome fact that God is involved with all things, including life, health, and happiness, but also with suffering and death. Visitors present for such occasions were touched by the very honesty with which Christians admitted that they do not always understand God. We do not have all the answers. A community that is *real* is attractive.

- Pray for deliverance.

This is a delicate area perhaps better handled in the previous chapter, in which we raised the topic in connection with the passage from James 5 (see pp. 77-79). However, many members are involved with prayers for deliverance, often even more so than the leaders. They tend to be openly aware of the reality of the evil one and Satan's destructive work in individual lives and relationships.

When we acknowledge that miracles of healing do occur today and we pray for them, it is only a matter of time before signs of the demonic appear one way or another. Only when I was willing to acknowledge evil and the oppression of demonic occupation was I able to begin to deal with it. For the longest time, Satan's harassment was present, but it went undetected.

The more conservative evangelical and Reformed churches have avoided the area of demonization and exorcism. Scripturally we acknowledge the reality of Satan. We are keenly aware of the powers of enslavement, addiction, and bondages. But we are reluctant to assign responsibility for at least some of the brokenness to Satan. We fear that if we recognize Satan's work and call attention to it that we will end up glorifying him. C. S. Lewis warned of two dangers that Satan poses: first to glorify him with attention; second to ignore him and in so doing give him free, undetected reign in our lives.

Without going into detail on this rather common but complex concern, these guidelines may be helpful:

- The church will face more confrontations with Satan.

With increasing emphasis upon spirituality and various religious activities, we can anticipate greater demonic confusion and affliction.

• Satan is a defeated enemy of Christ, and his days are numbered.

For some Christians, dealing with Satan tends to become an unnecessary show of power and confrontation. When I discern a case of demonic control, I confront Satan with the power of the risen Lord and simply and quietly order him to leave in the name of Jesus. It is not our power or noise or conviction that moves or touches the evil one. It is the authority of Christ to which Satan must bow. Satan may try to resist and stubbornly hang on, but the prayers of God's people and the declared authority of Jesus Christ bring freedom and release—often instantly, sometimes gradually. Satan's message

A man whom I'll call Dave was deeply controlled with compulsive, suicidal desires, but the strange dilemma was that he really did not want to die. Dave came to me for help to turn aside this overwhelming desire to kill himself and to do so violently. Dave daydreamed about driving his car at a high speed over a cliff or into a bank. He had already picked some locations. He visualized what it would be like to die from exhaust fumes. He talked about how people would act at his funeral. That talk would be interspersed with comments about his own "sick, repulsive thinking." Dave seemed helpless to stop it, and in his desperation shouted, "Help me, I don't want to be this way!"

After several such sessions, I became fearful. I sensed his awesome oppression, and no matter what I said or did, no progress was made. I was sure that anytime the call would come saying, "Dave is gone!" One evening in desperation, I called several elders who happened to be at church to join me. We met with Dave and after sharing his pain we began to pray with him. I had done that many times before, but this time Dave began to groan, choke, and cough. I invited him to repeat statements after me while praying, as I often do. I started by saying, "I love you, Jesus, and desire to serve you." With a hard, raspy voice Dave said, "I don't want to say that!" His teeth began to grind and became clenched together. His body became rigid, and more deep, throaty groans came out. By then it was obvious that we were dealing with the demonic. After at least a half an hour of intense prayer and rebuking in the name of Jesus, Dave began to relax. He was totally exhausted, but for the first time in a long time he felt that he was free. Dave told us he had stashed away two hundred books on witchcraft and the occult in his garage. The next day, he burned them in a bonfire that smoldered and smoked for three days. The desire for suicide never returned.

—Henry Wildeboer

of fear, defeat, and shame that has constantly played in the person's mind must be replaced with the biblical message that one is a new creation in Christ.

• Wherever Satan is active, he deceives and prefers to travel incognito.

Satan is most effective when not recognized. When dealing with a stubborn sin or deeply rooted pain or wound, one might well pray for discernment and ask questions. Has there been involvement with occult, seances, or long-term drug or alcohol addiction? When leading in prayer, ask the suffering individual to pray as well. If that is hard, lead with specific sentences like: "I love you, Lord, and ask you to be Lord over every part of my life." Such statements have a way of bringing to the surface the presence of the demonic. Satan, the lover of lies, hates love for Jesus in any form.

In orderly evangelical and Reformed churches, healing ministries—especially exorcisms—are often associated with fringe areas of the Christian church. It is not part of our more sophisticated congregational life. For many generations, healings and exorcisms were associated with inner-city, store-front Pentecostal churches where maximum ardor and minimum order prevailed. Where orderliness takes top priority, where spontaneity is feared, and where disorderliness is a threat, miracles and healings rarely occur.

Carefully planned worship services, though often beautiful, can be so controlling that at times they thwart the work of the Holy Spirit. Leadership sensitive to the Spirit's work will plan some "structured" spontaneity and discern when a change of plans is needed. In this open setting, we need not be surprised to see the Spirit move in mysterious, but beautiful, ways. When we open up our services to allow the refreshing wind of the Spirit to breathe new life into our worship, we give ourselves every opportunity to allow God's Spirit to surprise us. Miracles happen where they are expected!

A CONCLUDING CONFESSION

The writing of this book has been a major process, taking far more thought and time than I had anticipated when first asked to do this. The theological sections developed rather quickly. Miracles and healings are not objective issues for me, nor for the church. A long struggle has been associated with the subject. It is now also left in the reader's lap. You are now faced with the inevitable question: "What do I do with the issue of miracles today and specifically with my Christian faith and healing?" The answer calls for more than theological reflection. It is a faith issue. To believe is to think—but also to act and take risks. It involves one's intimate walk with God.

Looking back now, I acknowledge brief times of effectiveness in a ministry that involved prayer for healing and wholeness. The hand of the Lord has not been shortened; the great works of Jesus *do* still happen! But long spans of seemingly ineffective prayer also come to mind. I sometimes think of what might have been had I not been so cautious and fearful much of the time. That thought creates a sense of sadness. That others move into these areas with great caution and reluctance is quite understandable but also regrettable, nevertheless.

Equipped with a theology that wondered whether miracles happen today, and struggling for self-acceptance, I developed a diligent ministry that minimized risk-taking. Driven by fear rather than by the love of God, I worked hard tending toward perfectionism. When we allow for few mistakes, we fail to consider new ventures. "Safe" ministries and a driven life become the order of the day. Stepping out in faith that expects God to heal someone with cancer, restore sight to a woman who cannot see, or allow a man who was crippled to walk simply does not fit in.

Now I know that God loves me *even though* he knows me! The more confident I am of this, the better my self-esteem. The better my self-esteem, the more willing I am to be creative and take risks. Assurance of God's love lies at the very heart of faith, confidence, and courage. A growing, deepening faith in God is essential to beginning any kind of ministry in the area of healing, and no amount of book writing can bring that about in itself. We need to be motivated to step out and to proceed in faith, realizing that we will make some mistakes.

When we are laughed at and ridiculed for trying something new, it means learning to say, "So what?" When we are brittle and insecure, we fear such ridicule and criticism. It is all taken personally and painfully, every word a barb pricking the soul to the very core of our being. It hurts. Whatever hurts, we avoid, if at all possible.

Because that is true for me, I concluded that it just might be true for others as well. If so, it is essential to teach God's people to know firmly who we really are in Christ. Jesus is the very essence of our self-image. As we realize more and more that our behavior does not shape, color, decrease, or increase Christ's love for us, we can be more creative and take risks.

What is God's will for us in this area? How does God want us to deal with illness? It is good to pray. We have always done that, alone and with others. We have pleaded with God. No problem. But does the New Testament call for more? Are we called to *expect and act* in faith? Does God want us to declare, "In the name of Jesus be healed"? The few times when I have done so, amazing results appeared. But it is scary—I felt far out on the end of the limb. Big "what ifs?" arose in my mind. If you enter this ministry, you may well face the same questions.

A unified church with a healthy vitality is where the Spirit is most free to act. When a church is tense or divided, ministries tend to be safe and traditional. Risk-taking may create more controversy—something a divided church simply cannot afford. Members of a church in conflict feel like children raised in a home where mom and dad fight incessantly. Those children simply will not take risks to draw something, to sing, or to dance lest they do so at a "bad time" and a parent lashes out with criticism, totally disproportionate and unrelated to the activity, but an outflow for the tension with which they have been living.

It is the same in a legalistic church or in a congregation tense with long-standing resentments and unforgiveness. These are communities where healing is needed but where that is unlikely to happen unless there is first a deep seeking of God, confession, and repentance. That will be the first healing! After that, other miracles will follow. To create that unity and subsequently develop courage and confidence is often harder than praying to God for a miracle. Pride really gets in the way. The church is in need of a fresh outpouring of the Holy Spirit that brings renewal and new life. This rarely comes without genuine prayer, painful, honest self-examination, open confession, and a willingness to change.

Where that kind of searching and renewal occurs, the healing of relationships—a first step—is often accompanied by amazing physical healings. That should be no surprise. Forgiveness of sins, the restoration of relationships, and physical healing are related to each other and thus often come together. The New Testament has examples of that as well.

To develop a ministry of healing is more than merely adding another ministry to an already busy church. It calls for introspection, examination of what one really believes, and risk-taking. The opportunity for conflict is rife. Because healing is so very much an aspect of the good news, the church must not avoid it. Set in a context of love and patience, diligent study, and tender preaching and teaching, with ample opportunity for questions and input from others, it will open us to what God might do in his church and among his people. God's promise is valid. God longs to forgive all our sins and heal all our diseases (Ps. 103:3).

BIBLIOGRAPHY

Adamson, James. *The Epistle of James: The New International Commentary on the New Testament*. Grand Rapids: William B. Eerdmans, 1979.

Augustine, *On the Profit of Believing*, No. 34.

Bajema, Edith, "Together We Decided to Pray," *Reformed Worship*, June 1999. (CRC Publications, Grand Rapids, MI 49560. 1-800-333-8300.)

Berkouwer, G. C. *The Providence of God*. Grand Rapids: William B. Eerdmans, 1952.

Brown, Colin. *That You May Believe*. Grand Rapids: William B. Eerdmans, 1985.

Calvin, John. *Institutes of the Christian Religion, The Library of Christian Classics*, Vol. XXI, edited by John T. McNeill. Philadelphia: Westminster Press, 1973.

Harper, Michael. *The Healings of Jesus*. London: Hodder and Stoughton, 1986.

The Heidleberg Catechism. Grand Rapids: CRC Publications, 1975, 1988.

Keller, Ernst and Luise. *Miracles in Dispute*. London: SCM Press, 1969.

Kelsey, Morton. *Healing and Christianity*. New York: Harper and Row, 1973.

Kraft, Charles. *Christianity with Power*. Ann Arbor, Mich.: Vine Books, 1989.

Kuyper, Abraham. *You Can Do Greater Things Than Christ,* An English Translation from the Dutch by Jan H. Boer. Jos, Nigeria: Institute of Church and Society, 1993.

Larmer, Robert A. *Water into Wine*. Montreal: McGill University Press, 1996.

Lewis, C. S. *The Grand Miracle* (seventh printing). New York: Ballantine Books, 1988.

Martin, Bernard. *The Healing Ministry in the Church*. Richmond, Va.: John Knox Press, 1960.

Martin, George. *Healing: Reflections on the Gospel*. Ann Arbor, Mich.: Servant Books, 1977.

Merriam-Webster's Collegiate Dictionary, Tenth Edition. Springfield, Mass.: Merriam-Webster, Inc., 1995.

Ridderbos, H. *The Coming of the Kingdom*. Philadelphia: The Presbyterian and Reformed Publishing Co., 1962.

Smail, Thomas. *Reflected Glory*. Grand Rapids: William B. Eerdmans, 1979.

Theological Dictionary of the New Testament, Vol. II. Grand Rapids: William B. Eerdmans, 1964.

Warfield, Benjamin B. *Miracles: Yesterday and Today*. Grand Rapids: William B. Eerdmans, 1965.